Sleeping Under the Tree of Life

Advance Praise for
Sleeping Under the Tree of Life

"'Out of the mouth of this holler,' Sheree Renée Thomas' *Sleeping Under the Tree of Life* springs to life—to give us life. Continuing the work she set out with her Dark Matter anthologies and her first collection, *Shotgun Lullabies*, Thomas, in this pristine, poised narrative of our beginnings, extends and expands the dialogic paradigm of an art form and genre the world is finally catching up to, to go beyond what Michael McDonald and James Ingram sing — 'Yah Mo Be There!' — to take us back to the future of an Africa that said/that says, as the Bantu — 'Nommo Be There!' In *Sleeping Under the Tree of Life*, Sheree Renée Thomas collages together a narrative of necessity where her full literary powers and prowess are on full display like a Dogon cup from an ancient river where we drink in the magic of winged words necessitating change, each poem and prose piece not lulling us to sleep — but giving us life, and making sure we stay WOKE!"

—Tony Medina, author of
Broke Baroque and *An Onion of Wars*

"Sheree R. Thomas is a hoodoo conjure women. *Sleeping Under the Tree of Life* is a book of story and poem incantations. Thomas calls on the ancestors, the spirits, and our natural Mississippi mud/ blood history to talk to the future. She tasks, thrills, and twists our minds. Her word magic feels so good in my mouth, I have to jump up and speak her blues, jazz, and warrior woman sass out loud! *Sleeping Under the Tree of Life* is a book to read again and again and again!"

—Andrea Hairston, author of *Redwood and Wildfire* and
Will Do Magic for Small Change

"Sheree Renee Thomas gives us a whirlpool of poem and story, a 'wild and strangeful breed' of cosmology that maps each star from Machu Pichu to Congo Square, from Legba to Medusa. Here in these pages is a ringshout around a tree of brown woman hands and riverbent fantasy, all quilted up in 'indigo/ and black silt/ twisting the thick strands/ as if starting a slow fire.' The baptism awaits, the water is living, and we all rise with the tide of these epistles from such a wondrous, ancient, future-bound poet."

—Tyehimba Jess, author of *Olio* and *Leadbelly*

"*Sleeping Under the Tree of Life* is a collection of tales and poetry reflecting the mythical origins of life inside the dream of 'trees, rivers, stars, blood.' Through Thomas' words every day birth, desire, death becomes a beautiful, dream-like dance full of magic, light and dark. We are shown that things are more than they seem and under the most common skin lies infinite power."

—Linda D. Addison, award-winning author of *How to Recognize a Demon Has Become Your Friend*

"This collection of vivid, intense and artful speculative poetry and short fiction is a journey through beautiful, treacherous landscapes simultaneously ancient, futuristic and of-the-moment, inhabited by deities, demiurges, and drylongso conjurefolk. These guides, guardians and shape-shifting survivors illuminate Thomas' meditations on the joys and ravages of history and the resilience of love. Sleep beneath this Tree, dream these dreams, and arise changed."

—Ama Patterson

"In *Sleeping Under the Tree of Life*, Sheree Renée Thomas finds the mythic grandeur in human frailty and apocalyptic storms. This is a book of goddesses and magic, of songs mournful and joyful, of restless trees and falling skies, told in a voice like a river's hypnotic rush. You'll welcome the webs these poems and stories weave."

—Mike Allen, three-time Rhysling Award winner,
Nebula and Shirley Jackson Award finalist,
and editor of *Clockwork Phoenix*

"*Sleeping Under The Tree of Life* is a powerful invocation by a literary rootwoman working with both hands, a fusion of prose and poetry that brings to mind Toomer's Cane or Jones' Corregidora, works graced with lyrical riffs like little blue bottles glistening in the sun. With this work, Sheree Thomas has attained a new level of artistic maturity, her unique voice, a Wanganegressian fusion of contemporary and the traditional, singing out in a mastery of craft and vision that adorns every page. Her poetry claims the reader long before prose narratives are introduced in a seamless weave working that boundary/fusion of genres where new aesthetics are born. It is everything a work of art should be, a challenging engagement with the human condition that will try your soul with moments of astounding grace. *Sleeping Under the Tree of Life* represents a new level of craft, vision and achievement for a consummate artist and cultural icon. With this one, Sheree Thomas' place is assured. When great soul meets great work, what you get is a thing of wonder."

—Arthur Flowers, author of *I See the Promised Land*, *Mojo Rising*, and *Another Good Loving Blues*

"In *Sleeping Under the tree of Life*, Sheree Renée Thomas has created a gorgeously mind-altering collection of poetry and story. She riffs off history like a Jazz master, while invoking a poly-rhythmic present shot through with prophesy. With pulsating word alchemy, she spins luminous imagery, astounding characters, and deep-sea insights. I say, this book will put a spell on you—change you, and rearrange you. Read it right now, twice."

—Pan Morigan, composer, *Wild Blue* and *Castles of Gold*

Conversation Pieces

A Small Paperback Series from Aqueduct Press
Subscriptions available: www.aqueductpress.com

1. The Grand Conversation
   Essays by L. Timmel Duchamp
2. With Her Body
   Short Fiction by Nicola Griffith
3. Changeling
   A Novella by Nancy Jane Moore
4. Counting on Wildflowers
   An Entanglement by Kim Antieau
5. The Traveling Tide
   Short Fiction by Rosaleen Love
6. The Adventures of the Faithful Counselor
   A Narrative Poem by Anne Sheldon
7. Ordinary People
   A Collection by Eleanor Arnason
8. Writing the Other
   A Practical Approach
   by Nisi Shawl & Cynthia Ward
9. Alien Bootlegger
   A Novella by Rebecca Ore
10. The Red Rose Rages (Bleeding)
    A Short Novel by L. Timmel Duchamp
11. Talking Back: Epistolary Fantasies
    edited by L. Timmel Duchamp
12. Absolute Uncertainty
    Short Fiction by Lucy Sussex

13. Candle in a Bottle
    A Novella by Carolyn Ives Gilman

14. Knots
    Short Fiction by Wendy Walker

15. Naomi Mitchison: A Profile of Her Life and Work
    A Monograph by Lesley A. Hall

16. We, Robots
    A Novella by Sue Lange

17. Making Love in Madrid
    A Novella by Kimberly Todd Wade

18. Of Love and Other Monsters
    A Novella by Vandana Singh

19. Aliens of the Heart
    Short Fiction by Carolyn Ives Gilman

20. Voices From Fairyland:
    The Fantastical Poems of Mary Coleridge, Charlotte Mew, and Sylvia Townsend Warner
    Edited and With Poems by Theodora Goss

21. My Death
    A Novella by Lisa Tuttle

22. De Secretis Mulierum
    A Novella by L. Timmel Duchamp

23. Distances
    A Novella by Vandana Singh

24. Three Observations and a Dialogue:
    Round and About SF
    Essays by Sylvia Kelso and a correspondence with Lois McMaster Bujold

25. The Buonarotti Quartet
    Short Fiction by Gwyneth Jones

26. Slightly Behind and to the Left
    Four Stories & Three Drabbles by Claire Light

27. Through the Drowsy Dark
    Short Fiction and Poetry by Rachel Swirsky

28. Shotgun Lullabies
    Stories and Poems by Sheree Renée Thomas

29. A Brood of Foxes
    A Novella by Kristin Livdahl

30. The Bone Spindle
    Poems and Short Fiction by Anne Sheldon

31. The Last Letter
    A Novella by Fiona Lehn

32. We Wuz Pushed
    On Joanna Russ and Radical Truth-Telling
    by Brit Mandelo

33. The Receptionist and Other Tales
    Poems by Lesley Wheeler

34. Birds and Birthdays
    Stories by Christopher Barzak

35. The Queen, the Cambion, and Seven Others
    Stories by Richard Bowes

36. Spring in Geneva
    A Novella by Sylvia Kelso

37. The XY Conspiracy
    A Novella by Lori Selke

38. Numa
    An Epic Poem
    by Katrinka Moore

39. Myths, Metaphors, and Science Fiction:
    Ancient Roots of the Literature of the Future
    Essays by Sheila Finch

40. NoFood
    Short Fiction by Sarah Tolmie

41. The Haunted Girl
    Poems and Short Stories by Lisa M. Bradley

42. Three Songs for Roxy
    A Novella by Caren Gussoff

43. Ghost Signs
    Poems and a Short Story by Sonya Taaffe

44. The Prince of the Aquamarines & The Invisible Prince: Two Fairy Tales
    by Louise Cavelier Levesque
45. Back, Belly, and Side: True Lies and False Tales
    Short Fiction by Celeste Rita Baker
46. A Day in Deep Freeze
    A Novella by Lisa Shapter
47. A Field Guide to the Spirits
    Poems by Jean LeBlanc
48. Marginalia to Stone Bird
    Poems by Rose Lemberg
49. Unpronounceable
    A Novella by Susan diRende
50. Sleeping Under the Tree of Life
    Poetry and Short Fiction by Sheree Renée Thomas
51. Other Places
    Short Fiction by Karen Heuler
52. Monteverde: Memoirs of an Interstellar Linguist
    A Novella by Lola Robles,
    translated by Lawrence Schimel

About the Aqueduct Press Conversation Pieces Series

The feminist engaged with sf is passionately interested in challenging the way things are, passionately determined to understand how everything works. It is my constant sense of our feminist-sf present as a grand conversation that enables me to trace its existence into the past and from there see its trajectory extending into our future. A genealogy for feminist sf would not constitute a chart depicting direct lineages but would offer us an ever-shifting, fluid mosaic, the individual tiles of which we will probably only ever partially access. What could be more in the spirit of feminist sf than to conceptualize a genealogy that explicitly manifests our own communities across not only space but also time?

Aqueduct's small paperback series, Conversation Pieces, aims to both document and facilitate the "grand conversation." The Conversation Pieces series presents a wide variety of texts, including short fiction (which may not always be sf and may not necessarily even be feminist), essays, speeches, manifestoes, poetry, interviews, correspondence, and group discussions. Many of the texts are reprinted material, but some are new. The grand conversation reaches at least as far back as Mary Shelley and extends, in our speculations and visions, into the continually-created future. In Jonathan Goldberg's words, "To look forward to the history that will be, one must look at and retell the history that has been told." And that is what Conversation Pieces is all about.

L. Timmel Duchamp

Jonathan Goldberg, "The History That Will Be" in Louise Fradenburg and Carla Freccero, eds., *Premodern Sexualities* (New York and London: Routledge, 1996)

Conversation Pieces
Volume 50

Sleeping Under the Tree of Life

Poetry and Short Fiction by
Sheree Renée Thomas

Published by Aqueduct Press
PO Box 95787
Seattle, WA 98145-2787
www.aqueductpress.com

 First Edition, August 2016

10 9 8 7 6 5 4 3 2 1
ISBN: 978-1-61976-111-7

Cover illustration: Blue Beak, courtesy Joseph Eze, Copyright © 2016

Original Block Print of Mary Shelley by Justin Kempton: www.writersmugs.com

Printed in the USA by Applied Digital Imaging, Bellingham, WA

Prior Publication Acknowledgments

© 2000, "Machu Picchu" appeared in *Mélange: A Journal of the Written Word*, Vol. 2.3 edited by Nicholas J. DeAngelis (Lancaster, PA).

© 2002, "Black River Ritual" appeared in *Harpur Palate*, Vol. 2.2 (Binghamton, NY) and received Honorable Mention in *The Year's Best Fantasy & Horror: Sixteenth Annual Collection* edited by Ellen Datlow, Kelly Link, and Gavin Grant (St. Martin's Griffin Press, New York, NY, 2003).

© 2006, "On Entering William Edmondson's Sculpture Yard" and "The Negro Section of Nashville" appeared in *storySouth* and were part of a series of poems commissioned by the Cave Canem Foundation for the Studio Museum in Harlem's 2005 exhibition, *Bill Traylor, William Edmondson, and the Modernist Impulse.*

© 2006, "Fallen" appeared in *Strange Horizons* edited by Susan Marie Groppi and Drew Morse and in the *2007 Rhysling Award Anthology.*

© 2011, "The Grassdreaming Tree" appeared in *Shotgun Lullabies: Stories & Poems* (Aqueduct Press, Seattle WA) and *So Long Been Dreaming: Postcolonial Science Fiction and Fantasy* edited by Uppinder Mehan and Nalo Hopkinson (Arsenal Pulp Press, Vancouver, British Columbia).

© 2015, "Visitation from the Oracle at McKain Street" and "Nightflies" appeared in *Mythic Delirium* edited by Mike Allen (Mythic Delirium Books, Roanoke, VA).

© 2015, "River, Clap Your Hands" appeared in *Stories for Chip: A Tribute to Samuel R. Delany* edited by Nisi Shawl and Bill Campbell (Rosarium Publishing, Greenbelt, MD).

© 2015, "Arachne & Medusa Jump Athena" appeared in *Circe's Lament: Anthology of Wild Women Poetry* edited by Bianca Lynne Spriggs and Katerina Stoykova-Klemer and *Revenge: An Anthology* edited by Tamryn Spruill (RoboCup Press, Los Angeles, CA).

© 2016, "Treesong" appeared in *An Alphabet of Embers* (Stone Bird Press, Kansas City, MO).

Acknowledgments

I am grateful to Joshua Gage and judge Kenji Lui for selecting "What the Map Knows" for Honorable Mention in the Science Fiction Poetry Association's long form category in the 2014 SFPA Contest. I would also like to thank Smith College and the Lucille Geier Lakes Writer-in-Residence Program, Chrysalis Theatre, the Tennessee Arts Commission, Cave Canem Foundation, New York Foundation for the Arts, the Studio Museum in Harlem, Writers Omi/ Ledig House, Blue Mountain Center, the Wallace Foundation, the Millay Colony for the Arts, and the Virginia Center for the Creative Arts for their generous support of my work.

Sleeping Under the Tree of Life
is dedicated to
Mama and Daddy
and Jacqueline and Jada
and to the Beyon'Dusa Artist Collective:
Andrea D. Hairston, Pan Morigan, Ama Patterson,
and Liz Roberts

Contents

1 The Tongue We Dream In
2 What the Map Knows
4 Original Sin
5 Sleeping Under the Tree of Life
6 Ruins
7 Repast
8 Unmarked
9 Burial Ground
10 The Silent Ones
11 Mama River
13 Rootwork
14 Highly Favored
15 The Nightflies
17 Fallen
19 Kneeling
20 Dawning
21 A River Almanac
22 Hurricane
23 Visitation of the Oracle at McKain Street
25 If There Is Darkness
27 Machu Picchu
28 In the Crone's Herbarium
29 Terrarium
30 Confess
31 Urban Blight

32 Dead Ends & Corner Stores

33 Testimony

36 Reunion

38 Arachne Star

40 Arachne on the Rebound

41 Diary of a She-Creature,
or the Little Death

42 The Silence Between Us

43 Arachne & Medusa Jump Athena

45 This By My Hand

47 Lucy, Betsy, Anarcha

49 Sister Fates

50 Medusa Got Game

52 The Sun Burnt Up and Other Reasons to Riot

53 Church of the Saint of Dead End Streets

54 Ring Shout for Survivors

57 Return Song, or Why I Went South

58 On Entering William Edmondson's Sculpture Yard

59 In the Negro Section of Nashville

60 Revival: A Gathering of Mosses

61 How Everything Begins

63 East Is Genesis

64 Splendid Iridescence

66 What Demeter Knew

67 Black River Ritual

68 Full Blown Magnolia

69 Treesong

72 Origins of Southern Spirit Music

77 River, Clap Your Hands

88 The Grassdreaming Tree

105 Tree of the Forest Seven Bells
Turns the World Round Midnight

The Tongue We Dream In

Our first language was wet
mournful questions rang
like falling stars
in red clay throats

No milk teeth to help
form words, our eyes
made syllables, cries strung out
on ropes of tears, thoughts
dangled on twisted threads
of hope

Our first language was touch
balled fists of unlined fingers
grasping for fire, tendrils of light
blazed in eyes, molten with liquid fear
skin pricked and pierced with
stories to be told, lives to unfold
through the dark tunnel of years

Our first language was song
a bell hangs in our hearts
rings with every bloody drumbeat
songs to reduce souls to ashes
and songs to sing them anew

Our first language
was wet touch singing
ourselves across the darkness
into life, in our dreams we sing
in the first tongue, the language
before birth

What the Map Knows

Worlds so vast
loneliness
without end
with roads named
after dying stars
for men who brought hunger
from other distant lands
bought bones
from other distant bodies
and fear
of the dark oak forests
that held each other up
knowing fire dreamed
of swallowing them
and the tongue of the wind
was the scattered nations
wrapped around their shoulders.

Then, even the manmade river
was not silent.
He cried himself back to warmth
but they called him ice,
cursed him when his grief
walked their new found land,
grief covering the silent houses
like a starry wagon's wheel.

They called them kindling, savage blood
as if words would make it something
they can hold
in open hands

plot a way to follow
across the widening sky.

This is the map of worlds, forgotten.
This is the new world without end.
Where forests have been
cut away from their trees.
Flesh split, the bones exposed.
These are the lines blood
could not pass.

What the map knows but cannot tell
is that a grain of dust dwells
at the center of every flake of snow
that ice is a river grieving
that blood lives inside
a circle of its own beginning.

What we know is this:
the first language is forgotten
but not dead
the first name is not the first
or even the last.

There are names each thing
gives itself, contains its own
dream for life
and beneath us
the order already moves
maps, roads, rivers, stars, blood
the lines are ever shifting

a forest burning
a river grieving
land dreaming
and blood waking up.

Original Sin

The sweetest thought must be
a pomegranate seed
or a plump fig, inside gold and pink
outside, purple and green
vines twisting and humming
with a dream, the sparkle
of tiny sharp teeth

Sleeping Under the Tree of Life

The dark drank Persephone
but I vowed it won't drink me
I mixed my flesh with the fruit of angels
spread the burnt sienna, blue, and red
with my iron knife, spread the colors
until each stroke was a delicate carving
short-limbed and thick-waisted
low to the ground, I reached for hope
ripened in my blood like those first fruits
seed and semen, the green twisting limbs
could not protect you from our Father's voice.
Now I paint you as you paint me
unbroken images we deliver to the tree's
brilliant roots. I've drunk the juice that spilled
from your chin, you've swallowed hell
and we will survive the fall when it calls us back.

Ruins

We are never far from ruin
like the great ants on the carcass
of an emerald-winged cicada
like a monarch butterfly
buried in the gravel and the dirt
like the green side of a hummingbird
rising into view, you lie back
and consider a future that hangs
low like the sun collapsing in sky
carrion musk exists side by side
the scented hollow breasts
and wanders in the deserts
of the world, where from each
grain of sand and lump of coal
is a diamond and a bone

Repast

A last rock-skip hurled across the river's cheek
sunlight carved into our skin, where sweat clings
and skeeta bites claw and scratch, branch and bark
turquoise dragonflies crisscross creeks and dry-hump air
the branches above our head slice the sun
into bright gold bars that fall across
our faces like new scriptures in skin
and shimmer like flat green snakes and lizards
across the screen door and the porch floor
where our tired feet grip the black ribs
of wood and silence rolls across
our lips like oil across the wide green water
spirits will rise and fret
the mourners done already wept
the baked chicken is cold
we in our solemn stance
forgot the last dance step
is this it—is this what they meant
when they said grieve

Unmarked

Green leaves leap
through faded fences
crooked as snaggleteeth
the sky holds everything
but says nothing

She sees us climb, one leg
raised over the next
up and beyond the unwelcoming
signs, warning ignored
like the caretaker's advice
confusion in her face, a
sun shining in brown eyes

why would anyone want to visit here

A question our feet answer
digging in the dirt, the soil
and weeds spinning
from our heels as we
walk over the lumpy ground
and sit on sour earth

Beneath this abandoned lot
the state forgot, is kin
waiting in this lake of earth
waiting like a dream remembered
waiting like a stone turned

Burial Ground

The rising moonlight
climbs over the glass bottle trees
to rest row upon row
branch upon branch
above the cold flat earth.

And with night the watchers
circle the dead with a ring
and a shout that ignites the path
around a distant sun, here the spirits.

Rise and moan, call out
to loved ones long since gone
and wrestle while the fireflies
dance, above the broken
pottery, a favorite cup chipped
a tarnished spoon bent.

Navel names forgotten, they
wait for the wind to whistle
hymns, songs to soothe the
journey begun but not yet
over, no. It is not yet the end.

Here the spirits dance
their own holy step
wait to ride the wind over
the river, and that sound
over your shoulder is them
winging their way back
cross the sea.

The Silent Ones

There are souls who can take
a twisted limb, a diviner's stick
and point fingertips to water
trail or ditch, they can find the first
drops in the earth's throat
and quench your thirst before
it begins.

Some women can lend
the moon light from their
own shining foreheads
turn tides with the sway
of their hips, fishwife and
midwife to the ages, they
deliver loaves of bread and
seeds to feed the lonely before
night ends.

Then others can build shelter
from rock, draw comfort
from a stone. No patch of
earth can refuse to release
its fruit into her waiting hand.

You will know her in silence
You will know her in stillness
You will know when a star crosses
her full mouth. You're asking
questions, but she has nothing to say
because the answers are in the work
and the story is all in her eyes.

Mama River

Washes her hair
dark as the mirror sky
between her round palms
she rubs it with indigo
and black silt, twisting
the thick strands
as if starting a slow fire

Hair like braided
molasses, like split-fish
ends, stuck and formed
waterlily poppies
coiled and poisonous
as dark-mouthed snakes
roots deep as black holed
flowers in her red clay garden
tangled knots along her
watery banks, the ends
hard cattails, pussy willows
and bent Sunday morning
palms, her crown puffy as
rain-soaked mushrooms
black dandelions, sweet
as honeysuckle nectar
her kitchen like cypress
tree roots

I sleep on the other bank
one hand trailing in the waters

fingers bent, the other hand
combing Mama River's
windblown hair, her head
resting in my lap
the other half of the world

Rootwork

This is where I had my vision
sitting between Mama's legs
the braided channels of our minds
linked, like the thick plaits of hair
she grasped in her nimble hands
and oiled with coconut scented grease

This is where I bent my crown low
bowed beneath the ancient algorithms
passed down from generations
her hands hovering around my head
like brown cymbals, the roar of teeth
combing through wave upon wave
of electric black locks, the humming
sound another score to get used to

Back then Mama was Moses
her great conductor hands parting
my hair like the Red Sea
she was high bark and fat green seeds
she was red cinnamon dark and steady knees

I hold still while she scratches the surface
of my innermost thoughts, brushing aside
the doubts and fears with the back of her comb
they fall like gray snowflakes across a shifting sky
and when she is done braiding all the disparate
parts of my soul, her eyes swallow me whole
and her voice splits the air with her hushed breath—
that one shapeshifting word:
Beautiful

Highly Favored

My Uncle Larry sits Indian-style
in the crook of a storm-struck tree
his iridescent black hair shines blue
a trick of wavering moonlight
his cyes like smoke drifting

Perched there he hums
from the back of his throat
the sound like Otis Redding
He claps his hands and sings
jump rope songs to me
like he used to, testifying
about Miss Mary Mack all
sanctified and dressed in black

Fireflies blink in rhythm
around his head as he pats
the night air, tapping his own beat
as the wind whistles through
his belly drum, rattles the leaves
He says his head don't hurt
no more and he ain't studying
Vietnam war no more and
to remember not to forget
the hot sauce on my burnt
grilled cheese

The Nightflies

I remember the place
where nightflies sing like stars
their gilded wings reflect
the dark moon's glide
metallic shimmer, rhythmic hum
beat out a windblown pattern
foretell melodic monsoons
and electric rain showers

Always they came in the monsoon nights
the clouds angry and invisible
in the luminous sky, the submerged fields
lit by black lightning, its lingering
sulphuric smell a pheromone
the air heavy with the scent of storms
that do not break
the skies grown dense, exhale anticipation

And suddenly the night air
would be gauze wings, silent
inevitable as desire
how the light
caught the dark gleam of bodies
pale arcs plunging to fire
that brief gossamer blaze
like hearts that love only when burned

Mornings after the storm
my sisters would sweep out
piles of pale wings,
torn and shimmerless…

I remember the wet trembling
when we were like nightflies
blind bodies crawling
antlike in desperate circles
flung out in deep space
searching for the flame

Fallen

The night a comet
with its silver tail
tucked between its legs
fell through darkness
to rest in the Wades'
dead field.
Papa stood
on the back stoop
unmoving, wolf
starved in metal trap
teeth broken from winter's
harsh bite.
In the back of the shotgun
the crooked step jutting
out like a lip, he could see
the sky neck, feel the stars
shake they heads.
That night he threw
the fallen stone
back to sky
the stars watched
it all come down
to ruined earth again.
Sky would not take back
what she had done
the fields spent,
barren.

When the wagon wheel broke
shattered like Sis Bo
right knee, they fled
and Papa left
the wagon leaning
in the road.
The horse sweated
at high noon
the two youngest
on its back.
He shook its head
but not at the burden
the way Rushia
took the seed bags
the brown scuffed case
filled with the children's
best, adjusted
her Sunday hat.
Papa stood on the hard
packed road, stroking
the horse lathered
in froth, whistled once
and then the whole damn
sky fell on him.

Kneeling

When Grandmama
was gathered to her ancestors
we tried to hold her absence
in the space of two
steepled palms

We wanted to pray
but the empty house
on Randle had
long been a cathedral
of grief

The doors of the church
were open but
Grandmama
was already
gone

Outside her house
her favorite tree
felled, we kneeled
the seeds of the future
asleep in broken
pecan shells

Dawning

Something grows
in the sharp, brutal darkness
not a tree but its shadow
the wind stripping its bark
tossing its limbs, pulling its roots
through the weeds
light rises to the tops of stones
the throat of the lake fills
with the dark, slick skin
of time, the dust
of winged blueblack bodies
shimmer in the air
the sky breaks open
night seals itself and then
the sun

A River Almanac

The sun falls down with the grace
of a grandmama sinking into her
easy chair, who smoothes out wrinkles
of the day stretched taut across
her thighs and brushes the loose strands
of gray hair from her eyes. April,
and the river does rise. May,
and the cicada emerges
from the sleeping earth and flies. June,
wet and steamy, memory flows in deep
swirls and eddies. July, mayflies
and mamzelles dart and turn, hover
in the curtain of air where
the red clay burns. August, no relief.
The wind done gone and hidden
her head. The only shade
is the gift of trees and the hope
that Fall will soon rise from his bed.

Hurricane

the street is full of gods
night merged with day

sea merged with sky
the turbulent waters rise

naked trees dance
to furious music

wind spirits drift and moan
in luminous branches

stars circle each other
cosmic ring shout

repulsion, attraction
the force of nature
hurtles on

Visitation of the Oracle at McKain Street

See them l'il girls over there? Pants all tight and they
shoes too big?
Walkin' round here, lookin' like lumberjacks. Them l'il
girls
don't know nothing about nothing. They laugh
'cause my skirt ain't on straight. They laugh
'cause my lipstick crooked,
blackberry stain all around my mouth,
mascara clumpy, raccoon eyes
like I been stumbling in the dark.
They don't know I ain't got
no mirror no more. They don't know my hand
ain't steady no more, not like it used to.
My aim ain't steady but my vision still clear.
And I see all they see and more again.

I seen the water rise. Me, who come from desert.
I seen the wild and strangeful breed rise
from Abeokuta rock, wailing across the big wata
all the way down
in them burial grounds to 125th Street,
down Beale and Congo Square.
Last night, I sat on the levee and moan.
They don't know I seen false prophets rise
centuries ago, ain't nothing new
ain't nothing in ramblin'.
I been standing on these corners
sweeping dead ends since time began
since the river I drank from turn to dust
seen them write epistles in piss
carving curses in concrete

pimping pilgrims the pastime of the ages.
I seen the newborn choke on milk poisoned
I seen babies struggling against temptations
they ain't yet got teeth for
while you rush by me
frowning at my stink.

You don't know
this funk be spiritual
funktified force field.

Underneath this funk, a shield
frankincense and myrrh
guide lost spirits home.

See that girl over there? The one in the fur
knee-high boots, cussin' up storms? Like death,
it's hard to escape the laughter of children.
We will meet again, but she don't know that yet.
You and I will meet again, but you don't believe that yet.

You don't know these mismatch clothes
cover robes that got wings
You don't know this store front I lean to
be the city gate of the restless.

Simeon played the fool to mock the world
I play the damned, but you can call me saint
the big black dog guard the crossroads
I cover the dead ends, patron of the misguided
elder of the in between.
I cover the ones that ain't got but one option left.
But if you can call me by my true name, I just might let you
turn around and try again.

If There Is Darkness

The women carry broadaxes, side by side
they come singing spear to spear
iron striking cottonwood, cotton humming back
the waters churn, the pump and shuttle
sweep the warp like waves against greenlit shores

They come from the heart of it, each stroke
covering the space between, from where they were torn
to where they trained together, to where they must go
the women in step see only the next woman's back
together they live the story—a story of blood
the rising tide of iron, pummeling its way through flesh

If the sky's dark fabric is pierced by stars
they sing the songs of wombs, of the earth
giving birth to herself, of Herself giving birth
to earth—there among the green, twisting, fertile
things, they buzz with seeing, they blink back feeling
the wind and their weight of flat toes pressing into
 darkness
into the rhythms of the earth, they step, come, sing
 together
share the same breath, share the same death

The world is vast and wild and they travel
wary but with no fear, as they know none
have ever traveled alone in it, tethered first
to mothers, now they are tethered to themselves
to the sisterly beat pulse, pulsing in the next woman's
 heart

If there is darkness, they sing the light
They sing the songs of wombs

Machu Picchu

I traveled all the way to Peru
hoping to find a space large enough to contain
the feelings I hold for you

But

Dreaming
In Lima, Cusco
the Plaza de Armas
a vision stole down cobbled streets
and I followed it through the Sacred Valley's winding paths
across red clay and broken shards
of cracked pottery

Cut myself on the sharpness of your memory

Naked
Bathing in the River Urubamba
my blood ran cold in crystalline waters
as I washed away layers of doubts
caked on my skin like dirt

Purified
I climbed Machu Picchu
seeking silence atop that mountainous throne
but the ancient wind whispered
you
and as I struggled to breathe
amidst that forest of stone
the sun set on this truth:

Earth, river, wind
Love grows from ruins

In the Crone's Herbarium

Come, scatter of blue beads
with one hand I can reach for
a rootworker's last breath
caught in a blue vial
with the other
web spun of noise and scent
no marvels except those
reflected in my temple.

All the old stars aligned
do you know what to hope for?
Real nettles beneath the words
and invincible red root of the
burning bush, the seeds and
ashes of this world breathe
in a breath of green
then life remains, if not love.

And a question:
what do you see
pinned under glass
calling out to you?

Terrarium

Reflected on the other side of the glass
his back is a few flat acres of uninterest
his spine a ribbon of discontent, a river
that shudders in the muddy light
his lips are hunger, but they have long since
lost their taste for me, familiarity breeds
other desires, appetites among the weeds
and gathering branches, beady eyes and pincers
the currents of other waters, sweet and ever parted
and me, mute on a shelf, caught in a stone jar
contemplating the coevolution of flowering plants
the tenacity of insects, of evil joys and good sorrow

Confess

To wake in a still green forest
the scent of life as strong as sage
to walk among invisible gods
who still believe
is not purely a vision
but a command

If you cannot solve it
share it, if you cannot share it
swallow it

Watch its blood
leak through your eyes
spill from your mouth
secrets cannot dam the throat
forever, not even a stiff
cold drink

Urban Blight

Thieves press
through open doors
spirits rest
under wide-board floors

This is the way
of light and dust
that pools over
broken windows
the edges of memory
like forbidden thoughts
rising toward the apogee
of destruction

See the walls with
their gangsta lean
see the porches pout
and sag and scream

The slow arcs that bow
and scrape and leave
deep grooves
in the floor of our skin
and the years, like this street
all boxed out of sight
out of view, save for ours

Dead Ends & Corner Stores

Back on this end of the street
the one that jumps over
the railroad then jumps again
the black heat is a blister
on thc land, here the days
are reduced to artifacts and bones
Miss Ella rocks in a chair
shaped like a pelvis
she carries a jawbone in her shiny purse
and demons on a string of keys

Back where the cracks in asphalt
are sacred divination, where locksmiths
scoop up offerings to save the eve
and Legba guards the crossroads
drawn in faded hopscotch chalk
pebbles rest on heavy-lidded eyes
that watch you as you skedaddle by
talking about "hurry back now, we see you."

Testimony

I know a woman
who walk up and down
the street, calling a name
but don't nobody
answer back

I know a woman
who wear them same
mudstained flip-flops
a butterfly clip in her hair
calling a name
but don't nobody
answer back

She stumble over brick
and moldy wood
she stumble over somebody
baby-doll missing a leg
and wearing no clothes
no ribbons in her hair
she stumble but she call
keep calling a name
waiting on the splintered trees
to answer back

Calling a name
waiting on the split skull concrete
to answer back

Waiting on that warped front door
laying in the street
to open up
calling a name
asking a question
only she know
the answer to

In the morning
and the night
us wounded folk
stay close together
shoulder to shoulder
skin to skin
like our scar tissue
gon' mend together
like the world's glue
gon' stick back
all the broken pieces
of our life

We hold each other
try to keep our spirit calm
but the sky done fell down on us
and the streets crack
in two and somebody sang
a note from some ole
brokedown blues
singin' but they
blood ain't in it
singin' like they
chewing broke glass
and they tongue
just waitin' on
somebody to blame

We walk ’round here
kicking up trash
staring at rain-soaked catalogs
jacked up pictures
the whole world laying around
lying through its broke teeth
young women, used to be fine
fine! now they hair standing up on they head
now they staring up at the white sky
like they gon’ never love again
children eyes, lips swole up
like ain’t no laughter in ’em
old men who used to cut yards
stumbling through them
like they been suckin’ on crack pipe
don’t nobody see no future no more
don’t nobody hear nothing no more but
these brokedown blues
singin’ like there’s still
life between us
like time ain’t just
shut down on us
like these streets we live by
ain’t just fall away from us
like this asphalt ain’t tired
of this coming and going
this coming and going
like all the old potholes
ain’t too full of these
Katrina blues

Reunion

The years stain our faces
dark as the wet trunks of trees
in water the world breathes
in silt and fish
our blood changes from
cold to warm
yellow bones of spirits
shine from behind wide eyes
wake up sleepy cicadas
whose dry skins rest upon
the belly of trees
we stretch and open the
soft parts of ourselves
split like old souls
pecan shells apart
wear worry on our backs
like old women wear years
grace and resignation
yes, I am here, yes I am still
here, yes I survive, I thrive
we are all here

Something breathes here
life and all the stars between
under sleepy skies we rise
from the damp soil, cool waters
women, awake, girls awake
boys awake, men awake
the in-between awake
the beyond awake

the scales of our lives
rise and fall between joy
and our laughter together
is liquid amber
washed upon the shore
of shared memory

Arachne Star

Star weaver of tears
your memory-stained eyelids
hold in the fine spun night
you avoid the sharp
edges of shears
embroider time
with hair twined
from worry spells
heartstrings plucked
from the mourner's chest

Exiled from the cycle
of star and stone
you weave
a constellation of pain
the wind is your witness
and your unlucky guests

Artful executioner
how kind of you
to numb broken
and wounded hearts
with your poison kiss
we drift in silken
silvery sleep
free from fear
free from feeling

Only cruel knowledge
remains, the certainty
that our last sight
before the crush
of oblivion will be
your beautiful
lips

Arachne on the Rebound

It takes a special kind of stillness
a patience born of hunger
to live alone inside the matrix
of a cobweb

Inside, each strand is a harp
that rings silently, wet silver
vibrates with every kiss of wind
sings with each drop of dew

I listen with all my limbs
taste with a thorny tongue
desire and hunger fill
my hundred tiny eyes
all focused on
you

Diary of a She-Creature, or the Little Death

Grief settles on her brain like ash
pain knotted in a twist of spine
she rests on the skin of memory
a beast for the waning light
she circles dark rings of ruin
runs through the listening night
lungs strain for crisp moon air
the flight that ignites
knees, limbs, flesh
in the morning she is all teeth and gold
she digs into the wet soil of sleep
digs, dreams still filled with hunger

The Silence Between Us

Ghost laughter from the shining
folds of silk, we lie facing the past
black thunder at our backs
the silence more deadly than
words spoken in splintered thoughts

Arachne & Medusa Jump Athena

And it's about time, ain't it?

That girl always kept up some kind of trouble, always starting up some mess. They say trouble don't last always, but with Miss Athena, trouble was a never-ending story. What can I say? Some folks like misery and stress. Athena was that way, always up to no good, like to twist and turn things so that everything was about her. Had a real thing for victimhood. Don't get me started on Athena's tears.

Always got to be the finest one in the room. If you didn't know, you better ask somebody. Can't let nobody else shine. See you beaming, she gon' shade and block the sun. See you sipping cool waters, she gon' steal the drops off your thirsting tongue. Athena got to have the last taste—and hers better be sweeter. Or she gon' dry the well with barren sand and raid the river with a bitter dam. Poison is what she was. Killjoy, ain't got a single sister friend, the first. Only thing worse than a jealous heart is a wounded mind, evil enough to act on it.

First, she see Arachne, my right side, my *bestest* friend, minding her own natural business, weaving like she do. Spinning nothing but love. Arachne spins you dreams you want to follow, braid your whole life through. Hope in every glistening thread and strand, her splendid tapestries the work of a master's hand. But Athena can't stand to see nobody else's beauty but her own. She see mine and tried to take it. Thought a head full of snakes would erase it. Talking 'bout, *see who gon' want you now.*

Hmpf. Athena always been simple-minded. Her aim is sure but her vision unclear. She see what she want to see, and what she want is pain. Seem like everywhere she gaze, she see lack in herself, instead of looming possibility. She thinks beauty is what you see. She never bothered to look inside, to seek within, or she would know beauty is not where you've been, it's where you're going. Beauty is the life you make be.

So Arachne and me come up with a master plan. Athena was always terrorizing the land, ripping and running so, through the woods, taking lives with her tainted arrows. Talking 'bout, *bow down to the queen*. We wait 'til she deep dark in the woods. We wait 'til she can't see her way out, 'til she standing right where we stood. Arachne spins a web so pretty, it look like starlight, like great heaven above moonshine. A great silver mirror, glistening and shimmering in the shadowy night, even the fireflies stop blinking and hover in the hushed air, admiring its light.

Athena stops to stare. Now, she's the one that started that whole *mirror, mirror on the wall, fairest one of them all* mess, ratchet folks been trying it ever since. While she stunting and staring, Arachne's magic threads reflect the huntress' best self. I sneak out from my hiding place behind the elder tree, unwrap my hair 'cuz now it's *all eyes on me*.

We leave Athena there, a century or two, frozen in her vanity. Arachne gathers her webs and threads. I retie my headwrap and don my shades, while we laugh and laugh, dragging her name in the dust.

This By My Hand

This by my hand breathed

With the dandelion weeds
you dig and toss from your garden
I waved a fan, wove an arm basket
with leaves worked from earth
and dusk, brewed strong tea
my signature inked in the veins
and grains at the bottom of your cup

With the worn fabric scraps
you discarded, left to fade in the sun
grow mold in the open air
I sewed and stitched comfort
a rag rug of reason, a coverlet of care
memories to ward off cold dreariness
a quilt to hold off loneliness
when the world is without cheer

With the seeds you spat out
and left to dry on the paths
you tried to bar from me
I pieced together my own company
a ragdoll made from homespun
detritus, corncob and husk
a belly made from beans
where a future's hope
could spring

With the spices you could not name
I ground new truths and added
this land's ancient old grains
and mixed a fierce gumbo to
feed the dreams of a nation
not yet born, but whose hunger
filled my own, guided my hand
strength for an old one to carry on

With the dark clay beneath your feet
I kneaded the earth's blood like dough
coiled bowls, pots, and jugs imprinted with
my invisible lifelines and drank 'til I was full
with the knowledge that all this
by my hand breathed

I was here

Lucy, Betsy, Anarcha

—to sister scientists around the world

Three sisters
sitting at a loom

Are they sisters
because they sit   bound   together

Are they sisters
because they are   outsider   women

Are they sisters
because they are   un   named

Do they share
the same fate
due to a
coincidence
of birth, of shared
bloodlines

Three sharp points
                on an infinite plane

Fortuitous fractals
bones and flesh
of Plato's metaphor
Jefferson's dilemma
Sims' controversy

They are the sacred
geometry

Together they
define   our   world

In their fingerprints
the whorl of star-studded
galaxies
converge and align

As metal rings through air
hear the wail, see the stir of constellations
and know, whatever gods may shudder
our fate rests in their entwined hands

Sister Fates

Mourner, pick up the bones
you have buried. Fisherman
untwine the knots you have
tied. Elder, release the joints
uncurve your spine.

Time to do the journey again.

Anansi, retell the stories
you have told. Spider, rewind
the wisdom you wove.
Blues, unsing the sorrows
you scored.

Time to walk the path anew.

Sister Fate, unweave the loom
Sister Fate, remove the thread
Sister Fate, put down your shears.

It's not my time yet
  It's not my time yet
    Not my time
          yet.

Medusa Got Game

Listen,
with one look she could
snap the strings of life
turn you inside out
snatch you by your
shivering insides
put the crook on you
them two gnarly fingers
turned up like the questions
you don't want the answers to.

With one look she could
make you gulp air
through invisible gills
make you wiggle and twist
fling your arms out like you
paddling hard waters
drown standing straight up
on dry land.

With one look she could
cut off your head
and make you feel like
it *jes grew* brand new
make you shinier than
a silver dollar, make you
feel finer than a drop of
wine on god's top lip.

With one look she could
trim your fins, scale your skin
split you in the center, good and
dead and make you feel great day
in the morning alive again.

You know this, you been warned
you got a fi'ty-fi'ty chance
to live or be stone cold, so step!
But you willing to risk your soul
like all the rest, just to see
which look you get?

Might not be what she used to
but listen, that Medusa
still got game.

The Sun Burnt Up
and Other Reasons to Riot

Walk with me
out of the mouth
of this dark holler
we may never leave
this star alive
again

Church of the Saint of Dead End Streets

Save us from ruin, the great bell wails
each of us has something to sacrifice
something to survive

Ring Shout[1] for Survivors

Those who never danced
cross the edge of abyss
can never understand this
the serious love of living
how it's intentional *(like prayer, yes!)*
how you must be disciplined
(deliberate in the practice)
how you must do like
the Good Book say *(what it say?)*
forgive life *(forgive yourself)*
every day *(lawd-a-mercy!)*

Well, maybe it don't say that
but you can tell from
the heel toe shuffling between the lines
that's what is meant *(speak now)*
how you must find a way
to open your clenched fist
unhook the nails
digging in palm flesh
forgive the blood pumping
through temples and wrists
color in your own lifelines
and find a hand to clasp *(hold it now!)*
in your broken own

1 A ***ring shout*** is a traditional West African group dance performed by slaves and Black church revivalists in the South, where the dancers form a circle and shuffle counterclockwise, usually with a ***call and response*** song with hand claps and shouts. The form influenced jazz and is still present in some black churches.

(Listen) can't nobody ring shout good
all alone

For those who never crawled
and dragged their hollow spirits
back 'cross the dust, never looked in
and tried to turn away from the abyss
their elbows dark and ashy, fingers burnt
and nails jagged from the risk
they don't know about this

what it means to wake
each day and will yourself
to love life *(serious!)*
to live in the present *(say now!)*
to not will the clock's hands
back to chaos
to not will the clock to turn
in a backward circle of loss
of woulda, coulda, shoulda
until you don't exist
like the snake devouring
it's own tail, where the power
of old pains feels infinite
as hell

Time *(what you need!)*
to make your spirit
shuffle along when she want
to lay stone flat
to make closed hands open
like wild blossoms
with new seeds and reach beyond
the dusty fields of your mind
to shout *(shout!)*
to give voice to pain
and to dreams

To wake from slumber
arise and shine
to acknowledge and release doubts
to let your feet dance
to a strange, unfamiliar choreography
to translate gestures into ritual
to move your thoughts against
the lines of trapped energies
to dance in a furious circle
together, with other souls
flawed, imperfect
as frighteningly human
as your own

To defy
the dangerous rhythms only you feel
to throw salt over your shoulder
burn sage in every corner
of your wounded soul
to heal
and counter the haints
that would feed off
your worst memory

This is why we dance *(speak!)*
to defy and define
to repossess our own space
to clap hands and beat back death
with a mighty knotty stick that
keeps time and reminds us
we need not dance alone

Return Song, or Why I Went South

Because I wanted to be blind again
crawl through the caul they call
a veil and see again

Because I wanted to feel black
feel the darkness heavy and wet
and good all around me

I wanted to be held, like the night
sky holds the comets pouring down
the old bridge like rain

I wanted to feel the molecules of night
dance on my skin like the flutter of wings

Because I wanted to be where they
know my navel names, how to make
each syllable ring with sanctified country beats

Because I wanted to remember
the things I was supposed to forget
to learn them as blood learns the way
of sweet veins, as a river learns
the sway of its own banks

Because I wanted to fall into the muddy
waters to be cleansed again, unbury
the string beneath the tree, to be born
again, an old soul, alive and dark
bright with knowing

On Entering William Edmondson's Sculpture Yard

There is joy here

see it

in the curve

of a mother's lip

in the arc

of an angel's wing

in the trumpet

of a ram's horn

spiraling into dawn

silver strands of light

Hear them

chorals erupt

from earth's collarbone

there is joy

hear it

In the Negro Section of Nashville

Blood rises on hot summer wind
crepe bushes, honey petals trickle past
rough solemn wood
Inside your yard, the grass smells of heat
You nudge half-awakened stones
hands caress still curves, await birth
weeds spin in the shallows
gnats erupt on quicksilver wings
float on warm shadows
Chisel in hand, words are wedged between air
between breath, between blood
blow by blow, stone spirits rise and fall
softer than the curled eye of death

Here, the trees know how to wait
smell dust on wind and know rain is yet to come
You've grown lean, walking along
the city streets under a glassy sky
whispering to steps, crumbling curbs as you pass
stone for marrow and dust for skin

The wind sings strength
to your carving hand

Revival: A Gathering of Mosses

—after Robin Wall Kimmerer

I feel like moss on the back of a beetle
on the ledge of a cliff, I cannot compete
for the sunlight of trees, so I live my life
in the shade. I have no flowers or fruits
no seeds or roots, no support system
to hold me up. My leaf and stem and
every cell hold water against the pull
of sun.

I stand in a circle of daughters. The gaze
of our mother gathers us all in. When
the first drops fall, we are exuberant.
I dance in the rain of my sister's laughter.
A verdant reunion. Our spirits stretch
toward the sky, outstretched to reach
the rain. Cell by cell an unfolding begins
an overlapping as each stem uncurls.
Exposed, my heart is bursting with
change. I release my worries to the
rising mist. The air is lush and green
rich with the breath of mosses.

How Everything Begins

—after Joan Larkin

How the sky changes, the cloud
you'd skim from a pot of greens
comes clear, how laughter
bubbles like corn syrup as you heat it
how the eyes surrender their worry
a bright basket of blackberries
picked for cobbler, boiled for jam.

How flesh yields new flesh, lips
soften like soaked navy beans.
How the puffed skin settles around
a smile, sour dough becomes sweet bread
hot water becomes sustenance
salt and brown, delicate
and whole again.

How the dead hair, a nest
of unfurled dreams, grows
white, sleek, long, and reborn again.
How new thoughts like fire ants lit
a flame of feeling, peace with the past

How the shredded remnants
of an angry spirit worn down
and torn from its seat in the mind
releases new tendrils, plump
and tender, like morning dew on the
the first blade of grass.

How the old house with its yellow walls
of weary lungs and candle smoke
its peeled wallpaper record of the years
fills with moist, soft breath, light, hope.

How the breath brings its own healing
its song humming through all
the body's rivers and its banks
to the ark of bones beneath
the rounded breast, beaded and emerald
as a hummingbird's throat
hollow and light, the shadow and the dance
the gliding wings in the jewel-toned sky
to the quickening drumbeat
and the softening belly with its
navelstring and seed.

How forgiveness, how everything begins
hands unclenched, palms open, lifelines
revealed. How a mother's love
will lift the cage of bone, will lift
the high round belly, release the
tears of ages, roll the stone from
its entrance, and welcome the
revelation of life.

East Is Genesis

Wombmark of dawn
where streaked clouds
in lavender, orange
brush the world's edges
red birth of sun
dangles from sky navel string
its crown faces morning
striated light
washes rivers green.

Deep in forests
sound unfolds
slick green
of new leaf in air
the bright hair rises
through red clay:
day's first breath

Splendid Iridescence

If daylight is shaped by sun
and the memory of earth
is stored in Hades stone
then the echo of breath
under my heart
is the shape of you

Little brown head
curved, a copper nautilus
three swirls of dark
shelled curls, you
perfect in every way
like the vision I once held
in a desert of white sands
the bright mirror eclipse
offered a glimpse of you
but I was too young
to understand

A mother's love
as startling as glass trees
that rise out of the desert
like people, trunks and limbs
that shimmer and twist
bright tears reaching for sun

But the memory of your birth
cannot compare
to the story of who you are
and will become
a ray of stone, new breath of air
echo of many heart songs
and the future, a shard of light
this splendid iridescence

What Demeter Knew

Old souls reborn
silent on the eve of winter
carry the songs of spring

Black River Ritual

She fought the river all her life.
It cracked her walls, dug in its tongue
split them apart, swallowed her land whole.

She rebuilt them stronger, thicker
but it bit her ramparts at their base
spat lime-aged bricks as far as Somerville.

She dug deeper, lined up fresh river stones
poured concrete crossed with bone and shell.
Now she sits on her porch
with watchful eyes waiting.

I was ten years old when she carried me
to the mouth of the river.
Her hand—knotty fingers and a ring of gold—
hard on my arm, my shoulder.
It is always like this with families—
everyone involved in sacrifice.

She held me there
down past where the water turned
from brown to black to green
down through the rows of weathered weeds
the low branches of murdered trees
then up, wringing me back
one, two, three until I gasp
in the name of the father
until I am lost
in the name of the holy
found in this black river ritual
drowned then reborn in the lushness
of black river women.

Full Blown Magnolia

The sky was the rusted lid at the end of a tunneled night. The moon seemed lit by the light of bones. In her dream the trees drew in their branches, shrank into seeds. The child emerged from the darkness, wrapped her arms around the tallest in the clearing. The tree was the color of smoke, frayed rope, dead boll weevils. The child's favorite. She pressed her ears to its trunk, her face turned away from the wind, cheek against the peeling bark, listening for sounds dragged off like heavy sacks, bales of cotton.

Treesong

If you have a worry your heart can't seem to hold, take your troubles to the trees, my grandmama would say. That was in the Old Time, when I was a small girl with scraped knees and ashy legs, a neck full of sun. Her words would comfort me as I grew older, my baby fat yielding to strong woman curves and hips. Then I would fling my arms around my secret tree and whisper my sorrows into her knotty breast. This tree, elder of all elders, witnessed my most private moments, heard my laughter echoing through the years, and drank my tears salty with heartache. *In them time* I could peel back her bark as if stepping through a ringed door. On the other side of her silence I was stronger, wiser. I loved to hold her, to feel her weathered breast, a stillness against my skin. And sometimes as I held her, whispering quietly under my breath, I could almost feel her grow, could hear her sing. Her wooden flesh and knotted limbs moved beneath me, swayed and rocked me slowly, as if I were her own true seed.

Perhaps this movement, the secret language of trees, was my own creation, a product of my grandmama's lore. It was she who claimed that the trees that grew along the black ridge of her land carried secrets few would tell. That these trees had seen the first nations rise by firelight and storm, bursting from the earth's navelstring, had sheltered their swayed backs along a winding and rootless blood trail mixed with tears, had hidden ancient black seed in their limbs like some kind of strange, unforgivable fruit, had sheltered them and not swallowed their lives whole, as did some other bloodless trees, magnolia and oak, cold and less discriminating.

Grandmama said the trees that grew around her land were cousin to the Tree of Nations, an ancient breed who had walked with wooden limbs above rising roots and followed its people, chained and carried across the waters with only their memories free inside their heads. Grandmama said it was only these old trees who could move, pick up their roots, gather their seed, and plant them where they will, neither slave to the land nor beholden to the wind and her whims.

But I have never truly seen the old trees walk, though I have felt their movements beneath my cheek and their caress on my thighs as I climbed them. Perhaps they have grown weary of their journey, the people they seek now lost in a tangle of upturned roots and knotted bloodlines. Perhaps they no longer walk because the people no longer remember.

Or perhaps it is only the young ones, the newborn trees that are more active here on Grandmama's land. Young trees tend to juba and dance more than their elders think is good for them. Young trees have a secret desire, an inner ache that the elders forgot, lost ages ago, the urge dulled by time. And because this desire involves water, not rain or creek or the river kind that wanders around these parts, but salt water, the first water, a return is never spoken of. The elder trees disapprove of this waterlust and say, "the salt is treacherous, for it carried our people away and could not sustain us." But the young ones try to work themselves into any pool that mirrors the land, hoping it will lead them to De Big Wata and carry them back home to where the people remember their name. They move slowly at first, so the elders won't notice, then they stretch and whip and wiggle their roots until they are just about free, dipping into a stream during a summer storm or careening on their backs, swept by a flood at spring, telling all who will listen, river rock and stone, that they are moving, moving on, that the floodwaters will soon carry them straight back home.

On this journey, away from their elders' knowing limbs, some are dashed at the feet of mountains, some crash beneath the silent arch of bridges and are borne on the raging river's back to rest at the bank's knees among stones. Others, uprooted and ruined, dreams splintered and spent, become firewood to fuel new beginnings. But spirits unbroken, they sputter and pitch, refusing to yield to the fire's touch. And it is Grandmama's touch that I am missing, Grandmama's voice that was the last I heard before I went to sleep. On days like this, when I am feeling none too wise and very small, you may find me curled up at the base of an elder tree. She knows all my secrets, all the broken parts of me. There, I carve a moment from the everyday worries of life, close my eyes and reach for Grandmama's wisdom, close my eyes and listen for a treesong.

Origins of Southern Spirit Music

"There is no theory, you just have to listen."
Claude DeBussy

In a faraway land, far from a chosen people, was an old music man with a strange music shop. Shop was too kind a word, shed more truthful. But in faraway lands of forgotten people, sometimes the truth is best faced with a gift of magic. And where the music man lived, on the end of a dirt road that curved to nowhere, truth and magic, music and night, lived side by side. There, on the edge of the woods, the old man's little dirt road was the place where the forest skinned its knobby knees. It was the place where the river stretched her toes and the mountain rested its head as he drifted off to sleep.

The music shed was made of earth, river, and stone, and it was filled with the remnants of the offerings the forgotten ones salvaged. From the salvaged bits of metal and trash, the old man fashioned the strange instruments whose music was the breath of life. Some of the instrument parts he found, and some the children gave him. Whatever the origin of the gifts, he took the discarded bits of everyday life and wrote a song from them, made the doubters dance and the shamed ones sing, all sorrows turned to an orchestra of joy.

One night a series of pipes and flutes pierced the air, and as the door cracked open, a child poked her head in. She walked as if waking from a dream. Her hair fluffed on the left side of her head, a dark puffy frown. Tears glistened, starlight on cheeks that were full and brown. “Papa Othar?” Her voice was cool water, like the sound a mountain river makes when she wakes. “Mama sick,” was all she said. Water moon eyes told the end of the story.

The elder sighed, welcomed her with the wave of his dark, gnarled hand, the skin like weathered leather, tree bark split by the wind. His movement sent the golden disks and wind chimes to shimmer and wail, spinning from strings that dangled from the rootwork ceiling. The wind whispered in the corners of the room, set the water pipes to whistling. And the air in the shed vibrated like a one-string Diddley board.

“She eating?”

“No,” the child said, and stood weeping by the door. “She sleeping, say she not hungry no more.”

The old man lowered his eyes, nodded his head, picked up a vagrant flute, placed the metal to his lips, and said,

“Rest for the weary and souls too tired for a crust of bread.”

“But a body got to eat,” the child insisted. “That’s what my teacher says. To live long, she says a body got to move, and we got to put good things in it. Mama won’t do none of that no more.”

The old man chose a mallet and waved it in the air like a baton, then handed it to the child. He chose another and beckoned her to carry on.

In the shed whose walls grew taller, floors wider with each step they made, the sound of distant scales filled the air thick with memory and iridescent light. As they walked, the child’s tears formed into crystals, C-notes that shattered on the floor, beautiful and bright.

Together they walked with the strain of necessity, yearned for the strain of freedom. But the instruments in the old man’s shed lived by their own strange physics.

To the untrained eye, the shed was full of junk. But to those gifted with eyes that do more than see, to those who listened with more than their inner ear to hear, the shed was a wonderland, a black rabbit hole in a forgotten corner of the cosmos. Lyres made of garbage lids filled the room, and strange nautilus-shell-shaped instruments made from roots, designed to be plucked with fingers or stroked with a bow, dangled from the root sky. T-bars and wrenches, hacksaws and files, grinding wheels and gears spun like strange planets against the dark light of the shed.

Some of the instruments looked like great metal machines with teeth that could chew through any note. Others with buckets and pails looked as if only flowing water would make them go. Drums made from cooking pots and cymbals made from pans, dark blue glass bottles hanging from metal stands.

The old man, wizard and muse, was a master of chaos, drum major of dissonance, and the proud maker of many-stringed curiously harmonized musical things. He strummed a low harp with a satellite-dish body and resonator and plucked its piano strings, vibrating the pickup on the backside under its bridge.

Sometimes the river came and visited him. Sometimes she tap-danced on the roof, as raindrops from the river's bottom. Rain was another way the river chose to travel. She sounded out a symphony of sand and silt. She sang of all that she had seen in her journeys, of misery and mayhem, of courage and kindness, riots and revelations. She dripped, dripped her blues into the amber jug that sat on the highest shelf. He took a tree-trunk stump and climbed. Among his welder's mask and gloves, his wire brush and sandpapers, his bolts and bobbins, the old man found what he was looking for.

Held it in shaking hands, an instrument plucked from his steeple of dreams.

He stumbled over a spool of magnetic wire, caught his breath as he stooped to set it right. The rattle in the gourd creaked like old bones, the bones in his back creaked with old gourdsongs. Alone, he could fuss and fiddle endlessly, but the child's eyes and her mouth, a sad quivering O, reminded him that every soul arrived and danced at a time of its own. The song he would make night, the song he would make might hold Mama's spirit longer, excite the memory of appetite, remind her of the music that lived in blood. And she would dance again and hold the child just so, the puffy cloud smiling under her chin, but when the time came, not even spirit music could stop the will to go.

And no matter how sweet, every song must end.

Harp in hand, the old man climbed down from the night and returned to face the little one whose eyes were now a shroud. The child had walked past the shekeres decorated in bottle caps and net, past the lunch pail lutes and the shimmie-she-wobble flutes.

The child stood before a great giant balafon made of dried gourds and lost and found keys. She held the mallet high like a fist and struck each note with the strength of her fear. The sound of her grief made the old man tremble and shake, made him clutch the harp because he could not shut his ears. The keys rose and fell, rolled like a silver river, the crescent moon's smile. He waited until the child grew worn and weary, until her arms grew heavy, the balafon silent, and her tears spent.

"Here, dear one. Play this with all you feel inside, and Mama will hear your song, even in her dreams, where she now resides."

"And will she dance?" the child asked, and she took the bone harp and placed it to her mouth.

"You tell me, child, you tell me."

In her song he could hear the motion of waters and the play of curves in the evening breeze. As she walked away, blowing gently into the mouth harp, the wind lifted the dust around her feet and carried her song into the trees, beyond the sleepy mountain and the rambling river: if music is the space between the notes, then love is the space between lives.

And so it is, and so it was, in a forgotten land of faraway people, where music is the breath of life.

River, Clap Your Hands

Night

All night long, the weary sound of water dripped from the roof into the bucket below, eroding her dreams. Ava woke from a sleep that bore her like an ocean, her mind still filled with the raindrop drum. The moon had veiled its face so that the stars could not see her cry. She woke and saw the street alive. She remembered when the neighborhood was submerged. She remembered when she was ruined by waters, ruined and resurrected by waters that bore spent seeds, the corpses of trees, and times that would never come again. Neither born nor named, time swam lifeless inside her, and the lifeless tides swam with her. Ava touched damp garments that clung to her skin, close as guilt.

Watching the early morning walkers with their dogs at their sides, Ava was reminded that she lived among a people who believed in seasons. She lived among those who believed in the story and the song, among people who believed in prayer. Yet she knew nothing but the language of loss in a landscape she no longer recognized.

Ava rubbed her palm across the empty bowl of her stomach. Now she longed for the days when she had felt full, when the nausea filled her and all she could taste was the salt from the stale crackers she nibbled on. Longing gnawed at her brain, consumed her waking thoughts. She never had the chance to hold it.

Rain

Rain made her anxious. The river swelling outside beyond the bluff filled Ava with dread. The rain fell faster, harder than it had last night. Outside, the walkers had long since scattered. Only the hardcore remained, refused to retreat. All was a sheet of gray steel. Inside, her mind was pitch black, except the brief flashes of light that stung the sky of memory. The couple who came for her, flashlights in hand, the beams reflecting off the violent waters that careened outside her door. Paralyzed, her body was caught in between. Trapped between a birth and a transformation. The old house had become a ship, tossed along the siren's song. Long after, terror filled her, even on the brightest days, flashbacks of all that she had lost. She was weary, tired of losing what she'd never had.

"Maybe it's a blessing," Grandmama said. "Maybe the Lord didn't want you to have that child. Birthing in the middle of all that strife. The Lord spared him." Grandmama was convinced the child was a boy.

"You carrying that baby mighty low," she had said. But that was then, before the first gills came.

"Sometimes, I wish He had spared me."

Grandmama sucked in air, a tone to freeze eardrums. Her eyes were cool water.

Wine

She had loved him. Most nights Ava told herself she had. She missed the way his fingers traced her flesh, the way his eyes widened, marveling at her smooth palms and their missing lifelines. She remembered him tracing the curve of throat, him lingering there until she could not breathe, the simple pleasure before his tongue found the gills. He had drawn away as if her touch had stung him. She never would forget his fear staring back at her, pupils dilated in widening circles, receding like the ripples in the river, him pulling away like the tide of the sea.

That night she drank red merlot, glass after cheap glass, and listened to Aretha, feeling like everything but a *natural woman*. That night her mind was all rivulets and rock pools. She spent the evening ruminating, returning to the same eye of water. Ava added three teardrops of pokeroot to her glass, and felt her throat constrict and release. Grandmama's rootwork. She always had a recipe, but nothing could fix this—heartbreak. The flesh had grown raw and itchy inside, a wound that would not heal. Suddenly a soul in the lost and found didn't sound so unnatural to her. She had felt more than good inside, more possible with him. Now she felt undone, in flux. She was turned inside out. It was some time after the third or fourth glass, when the wine dribbled down her chin like ruby drops of blood, that she realized it was not his absence she mourned. It was the willful blindness that his presence helped her hide. Now how would she hide from herself?

Bridges

When Ava was a child her mother recited poems to her. Fierce poems of fault lines, of rivers turned, of a great tortoise whose back was as wide as the river's hips, of ancient paths lost and regained. They would emerge from beneath the Old Bridge. Together they dried themselves on the river's shore and watched the two trains running overhead. The air stung. It would take hours for Ava to perfect the rhythm of breathing. Sometimes drifters would leave piles of driftwood, old bottles, used cans. Her mother would make a fire and with a stick she would carve old signs and symbols in the soil. On those cool, mosquito-filled nights, Ava swatted flies and was warmed by her mother's company. Comforted by her mother's voice, her gills receded into her flesh, disappeared with the wind.

Mama kept her secrets close. Tight as water skins. "The Old Bridge is not the first bridge. Another lies in the water below," Mama had said, motioning with her hand. The thin membrane of webbing had finally dried and dropped away. It lay in scaly piles in the sand. "The first bridge was the river's spine, the Great Turtle. Our people swam across it, drifting finally into these waters. The first people we met lived up there, high on the hills." The high bluffs of the quiet river city were Ava's first glimpse of what would later become her home. Mama kept her secrets close. Ava learned this when she woke and discovered that she was alone. Mama had left her sleeping on the river's bank.

Hunger

When the river came alive, it hungered. It grew teeth and rose from its banks, swallowed the parks, the bending paths, the abandoned cars, the empty lots filled with broken glass, and encircled the bone yard, and the house. Ava woke to the sound of water running, like a faucet left on, and at first she thought it was a dream. She often dreamed of the river, the banks where her mother left her all those years ago, before the tall fishing man discovered her weeping by the still smoldering fire, before he took her home where she met Grandmama. But when Ava opened her eyes, she realized the water had joined her, and that if she did not rise it would cover her and all the room. Then the cramps came; thunder deep below her chest. The baby, it was coming too soon. The water had awakened it. The water called to them both. Ava felt the gills open on her neck, the skin lengthen and stretch between her fingers. She needed to get out of the water, she needed to resist its call. Trapped between the birth and her own transformation, she climbed onto the top of the desk, then took a breath, plunged into the water's oily depths, swam out the door, in search of Grandmama.

Hearts

It was the blame in their eyes that made Ava shun their company. The silent accusation made her huddle in the staging area on her own. People wanted to know why, couldn't understand how. The mayor said to go. Staying wasn't part of anyone's plan. "Why?" was the question that rested on everyone's lips. Why did Ava and so many others decide to ride out the storm? How could they not know the storm would ride them?

Grandmama once told Ava that her husband's heart had just stopped. "It knew Amp wasn't gon' never quit working, so his heart just revolted against itself." She said she found him lying on the floor he had lain down himself. "He came from a people who always used their hands. Sometimes," she said, "against themselves. But not my Amp. He built this house when we married, built it before your daddy was even born. I guess it's good he didn't know his boy wasn't gon' live long as him. In his way your daddy's heart revolted, too. Sometimes it ain't good to love so much in this world." For Ava and Grandmama, the house and its memories were all that they had left.

To keep the house when her husband died, Grandmama cleaned cracked china and porcelain bowls, shined broken mirrors and windows that stayed closed. Her hands cooked meals for dinners she was never invited to, graced tables with straightback chairs where she could not sit. Where she worked she heard haints in the halls and would return in time to make Ava's late-night dinners, telling her stories that left her amused, enthralled. She complained that there was nothing truly alive in some of those other, grander houses, the walls had veins with no blood in them. Grandmama said a house has got to breathe, got to have some soul and a little laughter to make its foundation stay strong, said not every house, not every family can carry the weight. She said what Ava and she shared made their home more beautiful, more sacred than the fanciest castle. Ava believed her, too, right up until the water came and took her past and future, her home and her baby.

Loss

Long after they lost their house in the flood, after they moved to another river city, Grandmama stood in line with hollow-faced folks. Worried and weary, she waited like the others to get her pills. The churches collected toothpaste and brushes, brought clothing and prayers. The kindness made the loss less sharp. The city's humid heat made them feel less naked. "But feeling clean don't help me sleep," Grandmama said. The water haunted her dreams, too. So she waited and swallowed pills she knew by color, tried to muster up an appetite to eat. Grandmama missed her garden and her homemade cha cha. Ava missed her baby.

Pain

When Ava found Grandmama, she was upstairs still asleep in her bed. The look on her face was pure disbelief. She refused to leave the house without getting herself dressed. "I'm not going with all my business hanging out," she cried. "If the Lord gonna take me, I am at least going to have on my good dress." The pain in Ava's face made her stop. "What's the matter, child?"

"The baby," Ava managed. "It's coming, I can't stop it."

"Stop calling that boy 'it' and come help me pull down this ladder." The water was rising up the steps. Framed photos, dishes, and books floated just below them. It took all Ava's strength to help her Grandmama up into the attic. The pains came so strong, she wanted to lie down in the murky water and let the flood carry her wherever it willed.

"Come on, Ava," her Grandmama said, reaching for her. They waited in the attic, darkness all around them. "We in God's hands now."

Air

While the water rose and their lone flashlight faded, Grandmama hummed and sang. She began with the stories Ava had heard as a child, the ones that told of a people who came from water, who lived and breathed it, the way the others swallowed air. The infant Ava had loved and feared rested in a worn sheet between them. Its skin felt smooth and warm to Ava's touch, but she knew when Grandmama first held it, that there was something wrong. The child, a boy, never took its first breath.

It was Grandmama who heard the people screaming below. She called back, thankful already though they had not yet been delivered. Racked with pain so deep it seemed to sear her belly, Ava managed to rise from grief, the blood slick and running down her knees. She took the flashlight and knocked out a hole in the roof. With each strike, the rain came faster, her tears harder.

"We're here," Grandmama shouted. Ava did not wait for the reply below. As Grandmama stood up, widening the hole with her shoulders and waving to the couple in the boat, Ava took the silent child, caressed its little winged limbs and released it into the water and the night. It was dark; later they would need a flashlight just to see the food they ate, but then, hovering in the house that was once her shelter, all Ava wanted was to see her child's face. For a moment Ava thought she saw the tiny body shudder as the water covered it. Inside she felt her heart revolt. *He came from a people who always used their hands. Sometimes against themselves.* Ava turned away, her face full of tears.

"What did you do?" Grandmama cried. Her eyes were fetid floodwaters, her voice cold enough to stop a heart.

Silence

The house they loved was a waterlogged corpse, but the city was not all they left behind. Something had changed. The water between them had darkened and risen like the river and the flood. They spoke in clipped sentences. Grandmama slept as much as she could, while Ava dreamed awake. She replayed each second of memory, trying to recall if she had imagined the infant wriggling, picturing if and how the child might have lived.

Thirst

The night rain came and invaded her sleep as stealthily as the night of the hurricane, Ava woke with a hangover and one question on her mind. She flung the coverlet back, placed one bare foot on the hardwood floor. Stood in the open door, wearing her good slip, wrinkled and wine-stained. She took a deep breath, inhaled the rain and the sun-shower air.

Grandmama had answered her call on the first ring.

Now, after making their way to the river's bank, Ava slipped out of her shoes, stepped into the muddy water. The river whispered around her ankles and her feet.

"Listen," Grandmama said. The weeds and trees swayed behind her. "The river is trying to tell you something: move, change. If your mama hadn't gotten lost, if she had stuck to another plan, she never would have met your father." Grandmama bent and picked up the shoes, wiped loose soil from the soles. "Here, at the riverside, is where they began. When she left the last time, she knew your daddy would return to the same place where he first met her. She knew he would never stop searching, never stop remembering. Sometimes it's dangerous to love that much."

Ava peeled off her dress and stood in the open air, the wind brushing her nipples, still plump with mother's milk. Her daddy had said she had her mother's face, strong bones, wide nose, wider forehead. Moon-marked, Grandmama had said, so she kept her in the sun. The closer Ava got to the river, the less air her lungs needed to breathe. She felt dizzy, her skin tingled and writhed with thirst. "Being lost helped us find you, Ava. You always thought the river took something from you, took your mama away, broke your daddy's heart, but maybe the river gave you something more."

Skin that was once dark and burnished now took on a copper-like sheen. Scales that were barely detectible appeared more pronounced. Ava began to walk into the waters, not far from the strip of sand where her mother had once told her lies and read her poems.

"I'm not mad, Grandmama, not anymore," Ava said. She unraveled the thick French braids she wore. Her hair puffed around her shoulders in a dark, wavy cloud. "I just need to try to find him. I know what I saw, know what I felt. I think he's alive."

Grandmama waved away a witch doctor that hovered near her ear. "If you're going, you need to listen to the river when you can't hear me. She ain't going to tell you nothing wrong. Listen to her now. She is telling you that there ain't no shame in changing. Baby, you are what you are. You come from this here water, but you also are part of this land. All them years I tried to keep you safe from this—" Grandmama pointed at the Mississippi—"but when I wasn't looking, the river come to take you back anyway. So find what you love most from both of those things that make you, and then you go on out in this world and make yourself."

Ava walked deeper into the shallow water, felt the river whispering, pulling all around her. Grandmama clutched the blue sandals, crushed the sundress to her chest. "You don't want to listen to me, then go ahead, listen to the river. It's been calling you since you were born. The water is wise. When you feel there ain't no other way, do like this river do and bend."

Grandmama stood away from the water, heels planted in the sandbar, as if she was afraid the river would rise and take her, too. Unwilling to leave on bad terms, but unable to stay now that they were good, Ava rushed out of the water to give her Grandmama one final hug.

And then, as if the sky had waited for this moment, the rain stopped. The only echo was Grandmama's whispered "Be good, girl. I hope to be here when you come back" and the hush of the river wind. Ava took a deep breath, inhaled the last of the sun-shower air. Humidity wrapped around her ankles, pulled her closer to the bank.

Sunlight shimmered

on the brown river's surface

the gold mermaid smiled

The Grassdreaming Tree

That woman was always in shadow, no memory saved her from the dark. True, her star was not Sun but some other place. Nor did she come from this country call life. Maybe that's why she always lived with her shoulders turned back, walked with the caution of strangers—outside woman trying to sweep her way in. The grasshopper peddler, witchdoctor seller, didn't even have no name, no name. So folks didn't know where to place her. For all they know, she didn't even have no navel string, just them green humming things, look like dancing blades of grass. They look at her, with her no-name self, and they call her grasswoman.

Every morning she would pass through the black folks' land, carrying her enormous baskets. These she made herself, 'cause nobody else remembered. And they were made from grass so flimsy, they didn't even look like baskets, more like brown bubbles 'bout to pop. What they looked like were dying leaves dangling from her limbs, great curled wings that might flutter away, kicked up by a soft wind. Inside the baskets, the grasshoppers fluttered around and pranced, blue-green winged, long-legged things. The *click-clack, tap-tap* of the hoppers' limbs announced her arrival. A tattoo of drumbeats followed the grasswoman wherever she went, drumbeats so loud they rattled the windows and flung back shades:

Mama, the children cried, *Mama, look! Grasswoman comin'!*

And the hoppers would flood the streets. Their joy exchanged: the grasshoppers shouted and the children jumped, one heartbeat at a time. The woman would pull out her mouth harp and put the song to melody. The whole world was filled with their music.

But behind curtains drawn shut in frustration, the settlers suck-teethed dissatisfaction. They took the grasswoman's seeds and tried to crush them with suspicion, replacing the grasswoman's music with their own dark song—who did that white gal think she was? Where she come from and who in the world was her mama? Who told her she could come shuffling down their street, barefooted and grubby-toed, selling bugs and asking folk for food? The white ought to go on back to her proper place. *But the bugs are so sweet*, the children insisted. The parents shut their ears and stiffened their necks: No, no, and no again.

But the children didn't pay them no mind. The grasswoman's baskets were too full of songs to forget to play. One little girl, more hardheaded than most, disobeyed the edict and devoted herself to the enigmatic grasswoman. Her name was Mema, a big-eyed child with a head like a drum. She would wake early, plant her eyes on the cool window pane, waiting for the grasswoman to walk by. When the woman would come into view, Mema would rush down the stairs, *skip hop jump*. Bare feet running, she'd fly down the road and disappear among the swarm of grasshoppers spilling from the great leaf baskets. The Sun would sink, a red jack-ball sky, and still no word from Mema. Not a hide nor a hair they'd see, and at Mema's home, the folk would start pulling out their worries and polishing them up with spite.

Running barefoot, wild as that other.

Her daddy picked his switch and held it in his hand. Only her mama's soft words brought relief to the little girl's return. Hours later in the fullness of night, her daddy insisted on a reason, even if it was just the chalk line of truth:

Where she stay? Did you go to her house? Do she even have a house?

Her dwelling was an okro tree. She laid her head in the empty hollow of its great stone trunk. Mema told them the tree was sacred, that God had planted its roots upside down so they touched sky.

Daddy turned to his wife, pointing the blame finger at her. *See, the white's been filling her head. That* tree *ain't got no roots. Whole world made of stone, thick as your head. Couldn't grow a tree to save your life.*

The girl spoke up, hoppers hidden all in her hair. *It's true, Mama, it's true. The tree got a heart and sometime it get real sad. The old woman say the okro tree can kill itself, say it can do it by fire. Even if nobody strike a match.*

Mama just shook her head. Daddy roll his eyes. *Stone tree dead by fire?*

Child say, *It's true.*

What foolishness, the mama say, and she draw her daughter close to her, tucking her big head under her chin, far and away from her daddy's reach. Then the man left, taking his anger with him, and he handed it over to the other settlers. At the lodge they all agreed: the grass-woman's visits had to end. They couldn't kill her—to do so would offend the land and the children and the women, so whatever was done, they agreed to give the deed some thought.

Next day, the grasshopper seller returned. The drumbeats-of-joy wings and legs swept through the air. Even the settlers stopped to listen. Spite was in their mouths, but the rhythm took hold of their feet. After all, that white was bringing with her such beauty none had ever seen. None could resist her grasshoppers' winged anthem, nor their blue-greened glory, shining and iridescent as God's first land. The sight was like nothing else in this new and natural world. They'd left their stories in that other place, and now the grasshopper peddler was selling them back.

The folk began to wonder: where in the name of all magic did she get such miraculous creatures? Couldn't have been from this land where the soil was pink and ruddy and no grass grew anywhere save for under glass-topped houses carefully tended by the science ones. They had packed up all their knowledge and carried it with them in small black stones that were not opened until they'd settled on this other shore with its two bright stars folk just looked at and called Sun 'cause some habits just hard to break.

And where indeed? Whoever heard tale of grasshoppers where they ain't no grass? Where, if they had already brought the most distant of their new land to heel?

The grasshopper peddler only answered with a chuckle, her two cheeks puffed out like she 'bout to whistle. But she don't speak, just smiling so, skin all red and blistered, folk wonder how she could stand one Sun, let alone two. They began to weigh their own suspicions, take them apart and spread them in their hand: could it be that white gal had a right to enter a world that was closed to them? And how she remember, old as she is, if they forget? But then they set about cutting her down: the woman lived in trees, nothing but grasshoppers as company, got to be crazy laying up there with all them bugs. And where they come from anyway?

Whether it was because folk couldn't stand her or folk was puzzled and secretly admired her strangeful ways, the grasswoman became the topic of talk scattered all over the town. Her presence began to fill the length of conversations, unexpected empty moments, great and small. The more people bought from her, dipping their hands in the great leaf baskets, the more their homes became filled with the sweet songs of wings, songs that made them think of summers and tall grass up to your knees, and bushes that reach out to smack your thighs when you walk by, and trees that lean over to brush the top of your hand, soft like a granddaddy's touch—land that whispered secrets and filled the air with the seeds of green growing things.

Such music fell strangely on the settlers' ears that bent only to hear the quickstep march of progress. In a land of pink soil as hard as earth diamonds, it was clear that they held little in common with their new home. And could it be that the grasswoman's hoppers were nibbling at the settlers' sense of self, turning them into aliens in this far land they'd claimed as their own? Or was it that white gal at fault, that none-working hussy who insisted on being, insisting on breathing when most of her seed was extinct, existing completely outside their control, a wild weed of a thing, and unaware of the duties of her race? The traitors who traded her singing grasshoppers for bits of crust and crumbs of food hidden in pockets, handed out with a sidelong glance, should have known that after all that had been given, as far as they had traveled, leaving the dying ground of one world, to let the dead bury their dead, there was no room for the old woman's bare-toed feet on their stone streets.

The head folk were annoyed at such disobedience, concerned at the blatant disrespect for order and decorum, blaming it on the times and folks giving in to the children's soft ways, children too young to remember the hardness of skin, how it could be used like a thick-walled prison to deny the blood within. Too young to remember how the sun looked like wet stars in morning dew, and how it walked on wide feet and stood on the sky's shoulders, spreading its light all over that other place. How it warmed them and baked them like fresh bread, until their brown skins shone with the heart of it.

But the grasswoman was overstepping her bounds, repeating that same dance, treading on sacred ground that she did not belong to. Not enough that her folk had stolen the other lands and sucked them dry with their dreaming, not enough that they had taken the names and knowledge and twisted them so that nobody could recall their meaning, bad enough that every tale had to be retold by them to be heard true, that no sight was seen unless their eyes had seen it, no new ground covered unless they were there to stake it, no old herb could heal without them finding new ways to poison it, now she had stolen their stories, the song-bits of self, and had trained grasshoppers, like side-show freaks, to drum back all the memories they had tried to forget.

Even the children, thanks to her gifting, were beginning to forget themselves. They hummed strange tunes that they could not have remembered, told new lies that sounded like cradle tales of old, stories about spiders they called uncle in a language nobody knowed, and hopped around like brown crickets, mimicking dances long out of step. They were becoming more like children of the dust than of the pink stone of their birth, with its twin Sun and an anvil for sky.

And a small loss it was. They had traded the soft part of themselves, their stories and songs, the fingerprints of a culture, for that deemed useful. Out went the artifacts that had once defined a people. Only once did they yearn for the past, when creatures could be swept away depending on their appearance. The grasswoman had even took hold of their dreams. The parents were determined to stop this useless dreaming. They knew if they were to live again, to plant new seed, they had to abandon all thoughts of their past existence. What they wanted were new habits, new languages, new stories to mine in this strange borderland in the backbone of sky. So the command was clear: the stone streets were off limits. You couldn't go out anymore. Curtains were drawn, and the houses shut their great eyelids.

Order seemed to rule again, but it didn't last long. That's when things began to happen. Doors covered with strange carvings and cupboards filled with stones. Furniture was arranged in circles and drawers mismatched and swapped round.

At the Kings' house:

Who been in this cupboard?

No one, none had. Grandmama King got mad: everybody in the house knew that her teeth were kept there. Now the little glass dish was full of stones, and from every shelf the stones grinned back at her like pink gums.

At the Greenes' house:

Who scattered grasshopper wings 'cross my desk?

No one, nobody, not anyone, none was the reply. Daddy Greene choked back disgust. *Grasshoppers all in my cup,* he muttered, *Damn crickets.*

At the head folks' offices:

Who let them bugs in?

Nobody had. The bugs had filled the bottoms of file drawers and hid in official-looking papers, fresh piles of pellets and grasshopper dung on settler documents stamped with official seals, the droppings among the deeds for land with their names scrawled across them like spider webs.

On the tail of all this, a general uproar gripped the settlement. The settlers held a straighten-it-out meeting, hoping to make a decision. They'd held off on the grass-woman's fate for too long, and now it was time to come to the end of it. They assembled at the home of Mema's daddy. The girl slipped out of her bed and stood at the door, listening to the groans and threats. She didn't even wait for their answer. She rushed off down the stone streets and slipped through a crack in the glass, in the direction of the grasswoman's stone tree. There, she found the old woman settling herself by the okro's belly, a dark stone cavern that swallowed the light. A great leaf basket rested in her lap. Another one at her side toppled over, empty.

They gone get you, the child say.

Mema was gasping for breath. The air was much thinner outside the settlement's glass dome. But the grasswoman didn't act put out. She seemed to know, and had gathered her two great baskets and released the blue-green winged things. But Mema could not see where they had gone, and she wondered how they would survive without the grasswoman tending them.

The little girl tried harder. She scratched her drumskull and tilted her head, staring into the old woman's face with a question. Never before had the grasswoman meant so much.

Run away, the child cried. *You still got time.*

But the grasshopper peddler just set herself at ease, didn't look like she could be bothered. Her hair and skin looked gray and hard, like the stringy meat on a bone. She pushed the baskets aside, pressed her palms into the ground, and rose with some effort. She stood, sucking a stone, patting her dirt skirt, and smoothing the faded rags with gentle strokes. Her hair hung about her eyes in a matted tangle. She seemed to be looking at the horizon. Soon the Sun would set and only a few night stars would remain peering through a veil of clouds.

Go on, child, the grasswoman said. *Fire coming soon.*

Mema hung back afraid. She glanced at the grasswoman, at her tattered clothes that smelled like the earth Mema had never known, at her knotted hair that looked like it could eat any comb, and her sad eyes that looked like that old word, *sea.* If only the grasswoman could be like that, still but moving, far and away from here.

Why don't you run? They gone hurt you if they catch you, Mema said.

The old woman stood outside the hollow of the tree, motionless as if time had carried her off. She stared at the child and held out her withered hand. Mema reached for it, slid her fingers into the grasswoman's cool, dry palm.

Mema, there is more to stone than what we see. Sometime stone carry water, and sometime it carry blood. Bloodfire. *Remember the story I told you?* Mema nodded. The grasswoman squeezed her hand and placed it on the trunk of the stone tree. *In this place you must know just how and when to tap it. Only the pure will know.*

The girl bowed her head, blinked back tears. The tree felt cold to her touch, a tall silent stone, the color of night.

Now you must go, the grasswoman said. She released Mema's hand and smiled. A tiny grasshopper with bold black and red stripes appeared in the space of her cool touch. Its tiny antennas tapped into her palm as if to taste it. Mema held the hopper in her cupped palm and watched the old woman, standing in her soiled clothing among the black branches of the tree. To the child, the grasswoman's face seemed to waver, like a trick in the fading light. Her skin was the wax of berries, her tangled hair as innocent as vine leaves.

Mema pressed her toes against the stone ground, reluctant to go. She looked up at the huge tree that was not a tree, as if asking it for protection, its trunk more mountain than wood, its roots stabbing at the sky, the base rising from what might have been rich soil long ago.

Can you hear the heart? asked the old woman.

The child recalled the grasswoman's tale. The heart-stone was where the tree's spirit slept, in the polished stone the color of blood, the strength of fire. Whoever harmed the okro tree would bear its mark for the rest of their life. Mema stood there, her face screwed up, shoulders slumped, as if she already carried the okro's stone burden. With gentle wings, the grasshopper pulsed in her cupped hands.

The settlers began their noisy descent. They surrounded the stone clearing, outside their city of glass. The little girl fled, her heart in her drum, hid, and watched from the safety of a fledgling stone tree. She saw the grasswoman rise and greet the folk with open palms, an ancient sign of peace. The curses started quick, then the shouts and the kicks, then finally, a stone shower. Tiny bits of rock, pieces scraped up in anger from the sky's stone floor were flung up, a sudden hailstorm. The old woman didn't even appear to be startled, and her straight back, once curved with age and humility, showed no fear. The stones came, and the blood flowed, tiny drops of it warming the ground, staining the black stone. They crushed her baskets with their heels and bound her wrists, pushed her up the long dark road. A group of settlers followed close behind, muttering, leaving the child alone in the night. The girl hesitated, her drumskull tilted back with thought, her neck full of tears. After a long silence, she stepped forward, facing the empty stone tree. Then it happened: the heartstone of the okro crumbled, black shards of stone shattered like star dust. She stepped gingerly among the colored shards. The dark crystals turned to red powder under her feet, stone blood strewn all over the ground. With a cup-winged rhythm, the hopper pulsed angrily in her shaking hand.

Suddenly, the child made up her mind. She dashed off through the stone clearing the children now called wood, crushing blood-red shards beneath her feet. The hopper safely tucked in her clasped hand, she noiselessly scurried behind the restless, shuffling mob of stonethrowers. Her ears picked up the thread of their whispers. They were taking the grasswoman to a jail that had not been built. *The well,* someone had cried, a likely prison as any. Mema shuddered to think of her friend all alone down there. Would she be afraid in the cold abandoned hole that held no water? Would she be hungry? And then it struck her: she had never seen the grasswoman eat. Like the hoppers, she sucked on stone, holding it in her mouth as if it were a bit of sweet hard candy. What did she do with the food they had given her, the table scraps and treats stolen and bartered for stories woven from a dead-dying world?

The grasshopper thumped against the hollow of her palm as if to answer. Mema stroked the tiny wings to calm its anxious drumbeat. Maybe the hoppers ate the crumbs, the child thought as she crouched in the blackness beside the old woman's walled prison. The well had gone dry in the days of the first settlers, and now that massive pumping stations had been built, the folk no longer needed stone holes to tap the world's subterranean caverns. Hidden in darkness, the grasshopper trembling in her palm, Mema began to suffocate with fear. The grasswoman had taught her how to sing without words, without air or drum. Was there any use of dancing anymore, if the grasswoman could not share the music? If the world around her had been stripped of its beauty, its story magic? And in the sky was silence, just as in the stone tree, no heartstone beat its own ancient rhythm anymore.

The grasswoman's voice reached her from within the well, drifting over its chipped black stone covered with dust. Now Mema could see the soft edges of her friend's shape, her body pressed in a corner of darkness. If she peered closely, letting her eyes adjust to the shadow and the light, she could just barely make out the contours of the old woman's forehead, the brightness of her eyes as they blinked in the night. Voices made night, is what she heard, felt more than saw—the motion of the old woman's great eyelids blinking as she called to her. The grasswoman's voice sounded like a tongue coated in blood, pain rooted in courage, the resignation of old age. Mema drew back, afraid. What if someone saw her there, perched on the side of the well, whispering to the unhappy prisoner in the belly of night? Footsteps called out, as if in answer.

Quickly, the child jumped off the wall and fell, bruising a knee as she crawl-walked over to hide behind a row of trash cans. One lone guard came swinging his arms and shaking his head. He leaned an elbow on the lip and craned his neck to peer into the well.

May I? the grasswoman asked, and she put her stone harp to her lips and tried to blow. But the notes sounded strained, choked out of her bruised throat and sore lips, where the settlers had smacked and cuffed her. The guard snorted, became suspicious. *Throw it up,* he ordered, and the harp was hurled up and over the well's mouth with the last of the old woman's strength. The guard tried to catch it, but it crashed on the ground. The dissonant sound made Mema gasp and cup her ears. *There'll be no more music from you, 'til you tell us where you come from,* the guard said, but in his heart, he didn't really didn't want to know. Truth was, none of them did. They feared her, the grasswoman who came like a flower, some wretched wild weed they'd thought they'd stamped out in that other desert and fled like a shadow, disappearing into their most secret thoughts. The well was silent. The guard glanced at the little broken mouth harp scattered on the street. They'd probably want him to get it, as evidence, something else they could cast against the old woman, but he wasn't going to touch it. No telling where the harp had been, and he certainly didn't want nothing to do with nothing that had been sitting up in her mouth. So he turned on his heel and headed for the dim lights down the street, leaving the grasswoman quiet behind him.

No, not quiet. Crying? A soft sound, like a child awakened from sleep. He shook his head in pity. He didn't know what other secrets the folk expected to drag out of their prisoner. She was just an old woman, no matter her skin, and anyway, what could they prove against the street peddler, guilty of nothing but being where being was no longer a sin?

When the guard's last echo disappeared into the night, Mema crept back to the well and picked up the stone harp's broken pieces. She held the instrument in her free hand and released the grasshopper on the well's edge. She half-expected it to fly away, but he sat there, flexing his legs in a slow rhythmic motion, preening. She clasped the harp together again, sat down on her haunches, and began to blow softly. As the child curled up in the warmth of her own roundness, she set off to sleep, drifting in a strange lullaby. She could vaguely hear the grasshopper accompanying her, a mournful ticking, and the grasswoman softly crying below, the sound like grieving. *Maybe*, she thought as her lids slowly closed, *maybe the grasswoman could hear it, too, and would be comforted.*

She awoke in a kingdom of drumming, the ground thumping beneath her head and her feet. The hoppers! Thousands of them covered the bare ground all around her and filled the whole street. Squatting and jumping, the air was jubilant, but the child could not imagine the cause of celebration. *The grasswoman is free!* she thought and tried to rise, but the grasshoppers covered every inch of her, as if she too were part of the glass city's stone streets. All around they stared at her, slantfaced and bandwinged, spurthroated and bowlegged. It was still night—the twin Sun had long receded from the sky, and even the lamps of the city were fast asleep. Nothing could explain the hoppers' arousal, their joy, or their number, or why they had not retreated in the canopy of night. Not even the world, in all its universal dimensions, seemed a big enough field for them to wing through.

Mema carefully rose, brushing off handfuls of the hoppers, careful not to crush their wings. The air hummed with the sound of thousands of drums, each hopper signaling its own rapid-fire rhythm. They seemed to preen and stir, turnaround, as if letting the stars warm their wings and their belly. The child tried to mind each step, but it was difficult in the dark, and finally she gave up and leaned into the well's gaping mouth. *Grasswoman?* she called, and stepped back in surprise. The drumming sound was coming from deep within the well. She placed her hands above the well's lip and felt a fresh wave of wings and legs pouring from it, the iridescent wings sparkling and flowing like water. The grasswoman had vanished; the place had lost all memory of her, it seemed. Mema called the old woman, but received no answer, only the drumming and the flash of wings.

She decided to return to the okro, the stone tree where for a time, the grasswoman had lived. There was no longer any other place she might go. Some pitied the grasswoman, but none enough to take her in—no street, nor house; only the stone tree's belly. As Mema walked along, the hoppers seemed to follow her, and after a time, her movements stopped being steps and felt like wind. It was as if the hoppers carried her along with them, and not the other way around. They were leading the child to the okro, to the stone forest, back to the place where the story *begin*.

Mema arrived at the grasswoman's door and looked at the stone floor covered with blood-red shards, the heartstone ground into powder. The okro was no longer dull stone, but was covered in a curious pattern, black with finely carved red lines, pulsing like veins. She stood at the door of the great trunk and entered, head bowed, putting distance between herself and time. Was there any use in waiting *for* the old woman? Mema blinked back tears, listened for the hoppers' drum. Surely by now, the grasswoman had vanished, taking her stories and her strange ways with her, a fugitive of the blackfolk's world again. The child took the stone harp and placed it to her mouth. She lulled herself in its shattered rhythm, listening with an ear outside the world, a place that confused her, listening as the hoppers kept time with their hindlegs and tapping feet. She played and dreamed, dreamed and played, but if she had listened harder, she would have heard the arrival of a different beat.

There she is! That old white hefa inside the tree!

Spiteful steps surrounded the okro, crushing the hoppers underfoot.

It's the woman with her mouth harp. Go on play, then. We'll see how well you dance!

They tossed their night torches aside, raised their mallets, and flung their pickaxes through the air. The hammers crushed the ancient stone, metal teeth bit at stone bark. Inside, the girl child had unleashed a dream: her hair was turning into tiny leaves, her legs into lean timber. Her fingers dug rootlike into the stone soil. The child was in another realm, she was flesh turning into wood, wood into stone, girl child as tree, stone tree of life. Red hot blades of grass burst in tight bubbles at her feet, pulsing from the okro's stone floor, a crimson wave of lava roots erupting into mythic drumbeats and bursting wingsongs. Somewhere she heard a ring shout chorus, hot cry of the settlers' voices made night, the ground fluttering all around them, the hoppers surrounding the bubbling tree, ticking, wing-striking, leg-raising, romp-shaking vibrations splitting the stone floor, warming in the groundswell of heat. And from the grassdreaming tree, blood-red veins writhing, there rose the grasswoman's hands. They stroked crimson flowers that blossomed into rubies and fell on the great stone floor. Corollas curled, monstrous branches born and released, petal-like on the crest of black flames. The child's drumskull throbbed as she concentrated, straining to hear the grasswoman's call, to remember her lessons, how to make music without words, without air and drum, and her thoughts floated in the air, red hot embers of brimstone blues drifting toward the glass-walled city.

And as the ground erupted beneath them, the settlers stood in horror, began to run and flee, but the children, the children rose from tucked-in beds, the tiny backs of their hands erasing sleep, their soft feet ignoring slippers and socks, toes running barefoot over the stone streets and the rocks, they came dancing, *skip hop jump* through the glass door into the stone wood, waves of hoppers at their heels, their blue-green backs arched close to the ground as they hopped from stone to hot stone, drumming as they went, bending like strong reeds, like green grass lifting toward the night. And that was when Mema felt the sting of blaze, when the voices joined her in the song of ash, and the stone's new heart beat an ancient rhythm, the children singing, the hoppers drumming, the settlers crying.

And when the Sun rose, the land one great shadow of fire and ash, the hoppers lay in piles at their feet. They had shed their skins that now looked like fingerprints, the dust of the children blowing in the wind all around them. And that night, when the twin Sun set, the settlers would think of their lost children and remember the old woman who ate stones and cried grasshoppers for tears.

Tree of the Forest Seven Bells Turns the World Round Midnight

Thistle stepped over an upturned root that twisted from the dark, wet earth.

"Your mama live near the river?"

"Naw."

"Your mama live in a tree?"

"Nope."

"Then what we doing?"

"Mama the river and the tree." She moved with deliberate grace, each footfall a code that unlocked another hidden key. Wilder should have known. Every other word out of her mouth was some strange, cryptic poetry. She was more siren than sage, more whistle than song. In the few months they'd been hanging, he had gotten used to her "magic woman" guise. Bohemian bruja, wide-hipped hoodoo. Unlike the other women Wilder tried to lay with, Thistle felt sincere. At least she was original. Most other relationships Wilder had had, all ended the way he felt now, lost. With the others he would soon lose interest—or they would, tossing him back on the street, the fascination over before it had begun. Then he'd be off, duffel bag in hand, looking for cover. To Wilder, everyone worked so hard to be just like the next. What was the challenge in that?

Thistle stood with her back to him, all curve and joy, a plum-skinned promise of delight. He tried to follow her, but his feet wouldn't move. With each step forward he kept stumbling backward, as if his body wanted, *needed* to withdraw every footstep, to retrace their path under that lone glimmering star. His car was locked and parked way down the road that flanked high above the river. If he hadn't been with Thistle, he never would have seen the trail.

"What I'm trying to understand is why we got to come see her in the pitch damn night?" He held himself steady, grabbed hold of a tender birch tree. All he saw was branches and limbs and more wobbly trees. Bark fell away from his hands in flakes, fluttered to the damp ground like layers of skin. "I'm cool with meeting your family, but why can't we go to Piccadilly or the China Inn? Don't your mama like buffet? That's what *normal* folks do."

Thistle turned her head, hesitated. Even in the deepening darkness, Wilder could see her eyes narrow into slits, her full lips poked out like she might offer a kiss. "When have you known me to be normal?"

Laughter shook the leaves of a mayhaw. Fireflies flitted a warning message in the faded light. Wilder didn't see. His eyes were in the future, back to the cool thin sheets in the rented room. The air was hot and humid, thick enough to slash a knife through. The sky was full, twilight now turning away from dusk. A super moon and that strange twinkling star Thistle swore was a planet. Which one did she say? *Venus.* Or was it Jupiter? Wilder used to know stuff like that, back when he thought it was important. Astronomy, astrology, tarot cards, and divination, none of it foretold anything close to what Wilder had come to know, his hard truth. Ghostly light shone through the waist-high grass, and the blossoming weeds cast shadows across Thistle's face, her arm outstretched to him like a luscious vine. This he believed in, this he could follow—the curved finger of flesh. An open palm, his favorite invitation.

"It's just a little further."

"I hope she got something to drink."

Thistle giggled, moved through the path, a silent wind. Wilder had made her a jacket with spikes on the shoulders and bright, colorful Ankara print for a lining. He hadn't sewn anything new until she'd tumbled into his life like a weed. In the black, weathered upcycled leather and the scraps from an old African caftan, she looked like the punk queen he imagined her to be. He had woven the jacket for her, his first gift, when she initially refused to go out with him. "I'm not fit for human consumption," is what she'd said. "Try harder," is what he heard. Wilder was persistent. He'd followed her, held signs at every protest, passed flyers out with other activists at the Riverwalk, harangued downtown hipsters who would bulldoze century trees for their new LEED condos. Finally, at a Mid-South Peace & Justice Center ice cream social, she relented. The jacket she donned like a crown. And she had worn it every day, her second skin she called it, even in the 105° heat.

But Thistle never sweated. A fact that startled Wilder, made him lie awake some nights and wonder, that, and her spooky, stony sleep. Gulping it down every chance she could get, Thistle drank water like a catfish, slept like an old dead log. But each time he saw her, a wildfire in his arms, remarkably awake, or asleep, corpse-like by his side, he grew more fascinated.

Wilder had met her at a friend's lecture at Rhodes on the music of John Coltrane, sacred geometry, and physics. Melvin discussed how Coltrane had composed "A Love Supreme" using African fractals and indigenous design, the same design found in ancient West African compounds, in passed-down rites of passage and patterns of braided hair, in the wooden sculptures of the Mende, in pine cones, and even in drops of water. Melvin was a philosopher, the baddest bassist in the world—*Time Out New York* had declared it, and Wilder knew from personal experience that to be true. Only one other bassist gave him a run, and she wasn't a bassist at all. She was a goddess; she was music itself, not even a fair comparison. Wilder had been planning to give Melvin the full Memphis roots midnight tour when he spied Thistle, fluttering in the periphery of the concert hall. Her back was pressed against the yellow papered wall, arms folded, as if she was too good to squeeze her hips into the plush student seating. Her eyes were closed, head nodding, as if she was hearing some other music beneath Melvin's words.

Later Wilder would learn she was rarely still—except frighteningly so in her sleep. Awake, she flitted through the world, an emerald-throated hummingbird. Even now she stooped to caress a crooked row of foxgloves. Her bangles stacked high up her arm like brass armor, glinted in the night. "Look how they bow their heads." She stroked the purple blossoms as if they were pets. "They're always the first ones asleep." She rose and darted ahead, a bejeweled black dragonfly.

Barefoot, Thistle used to collect ferns and moss and polished river stones, dark mushrooms and wild weeds for the birdcages and terrariums she hung throughout the city. She said her found art was a public indictment, a statement from the elders. Wilder never asked who the elders were. He simply chalked it off as more of Thistle's spirit speak.

So when she grabbed fistfuls of earth and held them before her nose, as if to breathe a prayer, Wilder only shrugged. "You should take off your shoes," she said and kicked off her boots, the tongues lolling as if they were hot and tired, full of thirst.

"Here? I'm not doing that." Thistle tied her shoestrings together and flung the pair over her left shoulder. The strings got caught in the patch of spikes. She shrugged, the leather jacket arched across her back like a pair of wings. "The earth is cool and damp here," she said and held out her hand. "Come on, every step is like a kiss." Wilder shook his head, no. She threw her head back and danced, her toes sinking into the moist grass. "Best massage ever."

Wilder paused. "I can think of better."

A sudden burst of wind carried Thistle's laughter through the air, lifted it above his head, lingered in his ear. The breeze felt cool, inviting. He sighed and unlaced one shoe.

"Got me messed up," he muttered and kicked off the other. He stuffed his socks in his back pocket, strung his shoes over his shoulder, and dug his toes in. The grass smelled sweet and wet, felt like heaven on his soles and heels. Within the circle of trees, he went beyond thought, beyond feeling. As his feet sank into the earth, he felt himself yielding to a soft green breath, a sensation he hadn't felt since childhood. He stood there, eyes closed, remembered what it felt like to run barefoot without worry, without fear. A deep presence filled the space around him, within him. Wilder glanced up, saw in moonlight the silvery threads of a webbed work of art, dangling from an elm. And like his lover, the spider was nowhere to be seen.

"Thistle?"

Only the familiar whoosh of the river replied. All he heard was the waves of the water, sloshing somewhere ahead, down below, and the sound of his own voice whispering in the waist-high grass and weeds. Slowly his eyes adjusted to the dark and the silver. The light was strange, as if waking inside a dream. Wilder followed the crush of green, where Thistle's hips had slashed through the ferny veil. Her footprints led him inward, deeper into the night where he didn't want to go. He walked in slow, plodding steps at first, searching for Thistle's trail, but each time he moved, he felt the air move behind him, only to turn and find no one there. Uneasy, Wilder moved faster, twisting through the rambling path, fighting the woods. He ducked beneath branches, cursing as he worked to untangle them from his hair. Instead of thinning out, the trees grew thicker all around. Wilder didn't like it here, the way the ground sucked at his feet, gentle at first, but more insistent with each step, as if the land was hungry.

He stopped. *That* was how she looked—hungry.

Those nights when he would wake, the room suddenly filled with the weight of a presence that made him turn over only to find Thistle lying flat on her back, hands at her side, still and cold, eyes flung wide open, mouth parted…

"How does it feel?" he had asked once, when the sun had risen and she moved, thankfully, once again part of the living.

"Like I woke up dead." Wilder remembered frowning until she kissed him. "It's like my mind is awake but this body is not…" Thistle often spoke of herself as if she was not part of herself, as if every day was an out of body experience and Wilder was her witness.

"Like you're trapped?" he'd asked.

"No, like I'm finally free." Her arms were wrapped around his throat, his head resting in her hands. She was curled beneath him, their legs entwined, her breath like peppermint and lemongrass, sweet herbal spice.

"But your eyes are wide open and you look…you look…"

"What?" She stared as if to dare him.

Wilder had searched for another word to describe what he could not say. *Dangerous* is how she looked, *feral,* but what he whispered then was "terrified."

Thistle raised one brow, rubbed her knee. "Sleep paralysis, common enough. I've had it all my life. It's like the body is paralyzed and your mind is still awake. REM atonia, when your brain awakens and your eyes start to open. You become alert, conscious." Sitting cross-legged on the rumpled sheets, she gulped noisily from a glass of water, then pressed a cool fingertip at Wilder's temple. "But then you realize you can't move, you can't speak, and you feel a weight pressing down on you, on your chest, and you feel like you can't breathe, you can't…"

"That's fucked up."

Her tongue darted out, licked the tip of his nose. "It's merely a question of transitions. The brain and the body, the spirit and the mind, move all the time, between state to state. Sometimes you are just caught in between."

"If I had to sleep like you, I think I'd just skip sleep."

"I don't sleep. I wait."

But she didn't wait. She'd left him, creeped out alone in the damned woods. And she didn't sleep. She didn't sweat. And when she did sleep, she looked wide awake. Dead. Thirsty. Hungry. The last few weeks she had given up her normal diet of vegetables, fresh fruit, and nuts. "What happened to the kale?" She had only shrugged. Wilder was relieved. It was as if his whole body was starving and all he needed was to nibble on one bit of bacon for release. He hated pretending, acting as if he was into all that vegan stuff. He had done worse for less. Hunger was something he'd gotten used to, a dull ache until he did some odd jobs or found a steady gig, or another cool-sheeted bed to lie in. With Thistle's new appetite, Wilder ate heartily, satisfied. He collected every meat recipe he could remember, and watched as Thistle sat eating strip after strip of barely cooked meat, mostly seafood, from the river that she caught herself, and piles of fresh water mussels with garlic and butter and white wine sauce.

Thistle was in a good mood these days, almost giddy, and she slept, if you could call it that, less and less. Wilder had started to think that this was one time it would be alright, until she had insisted it was time for her mother to meet him.

Wilder stooped to scrape a pebble from between his toes and rose, wiping a streak of mud against his thigh. When he brushed his hair out of his eyes, he saw a circle of stones. Wilder frowned. It was as if the trees had hidden them. One minute there was a wall of green, the next, a circle of stone. They rested upon each other like giant children holding hands in a ring. The wind picked up here, the air cooler. It carried the rustle of leaves and the rush of waters, the sound of the reeds clattering in the breeze, as if each were an open throat, rising to speak. Wilder wrinkled his nose. The wind carried a strange scent, something that made him wipe his face with his sleeve. Wilder had lost Thistle's trail. Instead he felt as if he'd stumbled upon an ancient conversation, the rocks and the grass, the river and the moss arguing about shadow and light. Wilder didn't like the sound, the sounds. They buzzed in his ears like static, a cloud of gnats. The hair on his arms felt prickly. He wanted to put his shoes back on, drive as fast as he could all the way home, but he realized he had dropped them somewhere back in the thickening bush. *Out here wrassling weeds.* And where had she brought him? Wilder felt as if someone had told him to drive to the end of the world, to drive and drive and when he got there, keep driving on.

Ferns and foliage had sprung up where he didn't recall seeing them before. The great stones seemed to rise higher, pressed all around him like a great crushing wall. The air felt old, godless. Why did Thistle leave him, alone in the dark in the middle of night, and who would choose to live in such a place?

He felt the slow shifting of eyes he could not see, then a sound like a bell, Thistle laughing, her voice high and clear. She was waiting for him, beside a tree just beyond the tallest rock, the one shaped like a raised elbow and a fist. A large web, the shape of a shield, sparkled in the moonlight, inches from his face. Wilder recoiled, waved his hand.

"It's bad luck to kill a spider," Thistle said, and she ducked beneath the web and pulled him close. Her voice was a murmured apology in his ear, as her nails scraped his jaw, razed the skin. Her ringed fingers ripped away at his collar, exposed his throat. Thistle tore off his shirt, kicked it into the ground that was covered in a thin layer of rising mist. She rolled up his tank, scraped at his back and neck, her tongue deep in his throat, stumbling through the tangled branches and moss-covered stones until he fell limp, into a bed of leaves, shoulders stooped, arms hanging at his sides. Tiny hot scratches scraped along the softness of his belly, down the length of his arms; a cut stung on his chin. Thistle nipped, nibbled at his nose.

As odd as she was, Wilder loved being with Thistle. He felt himself expand in her presence. Her strangeness and stories awakened in him a vague awareness of his own. It wasn't that he didn't care about the land or "her sisters," the damn weeds and the river, or whatever Thistle was always so amped up about. It's just that he saw the state of the world as out of his hands—something decided by others more predatory, more resourced than he. For Wilder, fighting was a losing proposition. Someday the meek would inherit the earth, but not in real time, so why spend what little time you've got, stressed? Wilder didn't want to make a difference; he wanted fucking change. When that didn't happen when he thought it should, he gave up.

A long time ago Wilder had had skin in the game. He'd put his neck out there, like Thistle, believing, marching, singing, guitar playing, airbrushing, phone banking, door knocking, and leafleting, only to have it crushed by the world, again and again. There had been some successes, but the failures were more than he could bear. The night Thistle finally came to him, he had marched with her and the others against the Stiles Water Treatment plant. Stiles was vile. It dumped partially treated sewage wastewater into the river, claiming rapid dilution by the Mississippi's vast flow and hiding under the cover that the river was used mostly for industry and commercial traffic. Thistle and the other activists knew that state law required all Tennessee waters to be fishable and swimmable. The only folks who fished and swam in the river bottoms were too dumb to know better or desperate or both. Or Thistle. Thistle painted a beautiful, huge canvas mural that had to be carried by twenty hands, calling for disinfection and respect for her "mother," the river. Wilder joined the protest only because he wanted to be near her. He wanted to show that he was willing to go wherever she was, that he was down with the cause, her cause, even if it didn't make much sense.

When he dropped out of school, Wilder had spent years on the streets lonely and hungry, and denying both while searching for truth in flesh. He couldn't find his tribe, but wherever he wandered, music was his solace. Wilder never stayed in one place long, never loved one heart long. He had learned to survive, to protect the soft parts of himself. But the world had eaten his spirit up and spat him out, left him pulp and gristle at Thistle's feet.

"It's not enough that I'm barefoot and getting eaten up by bugs, but now we've got to play hide and seek in the dark?" Thistle bowed her head, smiled. Wilder held her close, lifted her chin. Damp pine needles pricked his back. "You know we could have done that back at the house."

"Mama's not back at your house."

"Where the hell is Mama?"

Thistle pulled away and rose, turning her back to him. He stood up, wiping matted leaves off his legs. "What's wrong?" She didn't answer but offered her hand, her palm cool and damp. Wordless, she led him through an opening in the stone door he had not seen, her hand still clasped in his. As they walked, waves of coolness trickled between his toes, tickled Wilder's soles. He looked down, stared at the flat surface of the water. It stared back up at him, a dark mirror. A dense, blue fog clung to the trunks of the trees. Behind him, the old stones groaned. Up above, the stars revealed themselves one by one in the veil of night.

"This way. She's here."

Together, they waded through the river mud and muck. Thistle held his hand in a tight, possessive grip, squeezing his fingers with her silver rings, as if he might flee. She walked with her back to the darkness, her eyes willing him forward toward a tunnel of trees ahead. Her feet moved expertly, as if she had walked the unseen path a hundred times before.

"Slow down, Thistle, you're going too fast. You're going to fall."

"Hasn't happened yet." The hair bristled on the nape of his neck. How many times had she walked this path before?

Thistle's steps through the stream had become quick and light, silkfire dancing through the night. She moved as if possessed, as if each step were a key she played in a song for the earth. Wilder's footsteps were heavy and unsure. His breath grew ragged. Sweat trickled down his chest and back, made his skin stick to his tank top, made him wipe his shoulder with his chin.

They passed a stand of young saplings. Thistle paused to stroke their stalks tenderly, whispered as if telling them secrets. The wind rustled in a red maple's leaves. She tilted her head, as if to listen. Wilder sighed, swatted a mosquito that looked big as his hand. "Please, can we go now? I don't want to be out here all night, Thistle. I'm getting eaten alive here."

She stopped. He could hear distant voices, perhaps from a barge floating by. A muffled grumbling sound rumbled through the air, like the echo of trucks speeding across the I-55 bridge. Wilder frowned. The old bridge was too far away for that. "Let's hurry, then. You're more than ready," Thistle said.

"Look, we could be home by now, eating. I know you're hungry. You're always hungry these days. I mean, why are we here? Is this even necessary right—"

"I wanted to show you where I came from," Thistle interrupted. "Who I came from, why I am."

Wilder shuddered. His feet were cold. The drying sweat had chilled on his skin, but despite his discomfort, he accepted her answer. It was what he'd wanted to hear. For months she had been secretive, silent. If he hadn't seen her student ID, he never would have known that she had been working on her master's in bryology. Her thesis was on the role of moss in rejuvenating human scarred land, healing poisoned waters. "Ecological succession" is what she'd called it. "Every hour the Mississippi River Delta is disappearing; one football field of wetlands vanishes at a time. Your levees have strangled it, your channels and canals have allowed saltwater and waste to poison it. Whole ecosystems are drowning in muck."

"You think moss and algae and shit can save it?" he'd asked.

She'd nodded. "I do." Wilder had snorted. Thistle had sat back, watched him in silence. Maybe that was when it had changed. Her sleeping patterns, her eating, everything, even the way she looked at him, held him when they made love, before she drifted off into her open-eyed sleep.

Thistle claimed she already had a lifetime of degrees in environmental forestry and the science of trees, but moss was a new interest for her. The change in scale, she'd said, the smaller focus, enriched her life, changed her view.

"You have to expand your vision and make your spirit very small. I'm so used to being—"

"Being what?" he'd asked. She'd slipped the photo card back into her satchel. Her face was ashen, her lips a thin, grim line.

"Being rooted in everything."

Now she looked amused, almost giddy. She moved in an intoxicated sway, as if she was dancing to a furious music.

"Remember when you asked me about the others, the ones before you?"

"Yeah, and you said to leave the past the past."

She smiled. "Don't you want to know?"

"No, I don't." Wilder's eyes darted, like the fireflies that fluttered past them. He was starting to imagine movement in the dark. A rustle by that tree, a whispered hiss underneath a bush. He grew more unsettled the longer she stared at him, humming and swaying. "I know everything I need to know about you—don't need to know anymore—and besides, I've already met your mother. See," he said and stomped his feet in the rising water that grew colder, "the river. And here—" He leaned against a gnarled, narrow blackgum, so twisted it almost looked bent. "The tree. Pleased to meet you, Mama. Now can we go?"

Thistle shook her head. "If you core these trees, you'll find that some of them are over 150 years old. Or older, like that one there. So now you've met Loridant. He was one of my favorites."

Wilder frowned. "Favorite what?"

"They say he disappeared after he led an expedition here, when the Chickasaw tended this land, but I see you have found him."

Wilder jerked away from the alligator bark, sucked in air, steadied his voice. "Come on, where is she? I see you're not going to end this game until I meet her, so let's go."

He marched ahead of Thistle, snatching at branches that leaned in his face, swatting at the high grass, cursing the weeds that created a wall around him. *Why did he let her toss his good shirt?* His white tank top wasn't much defense against the scratches and the bug bites. It glowed in the dark, making him look like a ghost slipping through the trees. The air was more fragrant here, dark and sweet, cloying. He could hear Thistle giggling behind him. She was practically singing now.

"There better be some Fireball when I get there."

Wilder would have kept marching and cussing if he hadn't fallen into the marsh.

"What the—Thistle? Thistle!"

It was as if the land had given up and the river had taken over. Wilder found himself knee-high in a black bowl of muddy, sludge-like water, but it wasn't the water that worried him. The moonlight reflected an image so uncanny that it made the inside of Wilder's scalp itch.

Straight ahead, in the center of the circle was a huge cypress tree. Its great dark, tall plumes stabbed against the sky. Its trunk or trunks rose from the water in a huge entwined knot, covered in green fungus. It appeared to combine at least two other trees. Huge tangled roots rose in and out of the water, like knobby knees, a great serpent's nest. The limbs were massive and coiled in the air like mighty arms. The bark around its base was smooth, save for a series of fire scars, as if someone had tried to burn it, many times over. Standing in the shadow of this giant, Wilder felt as close to God or the Devil as he had ever felt.

Thistle stopped just short of the water. Her face calm, her eyes shining in the light.

"Mama."

The ground shook, rippled beneath them, and the triple tree seemed to bow in answer. *This shouldn't be here.* Wilder knew nothing like that grew in the area. Maybe a couple hours away in Mississippi, where the cypress trees in Humphreys County were some of the largest in the world, 97 feet around, 118 feet tall, the South's own sequoias, or maybe down in Texas and Louisiana, but not down in the delta in the mouth of the river in West Tennessee.

As if hearing his thoughts, the tree's great limbs bent forward, but Wilder did not feel any wind or breeze. Instead, the water around him began to warm and bubble. Water lilies with huge poppies bobbed and floated in the bubbling water. Wilder tried to back out, his voice lost in the rumbling of the strange tree, but something twisted around his ankles, held him in place. He screamed, fearing it was a snake, and reached into the water. Instead of scales, his fingers felt wet vines and scalelike leaves. He tried to rip the heavy vines off, his fingers digging into them. He yanked one and tossed it. It landed in the muddy pool with a splash, heavy as a walking stick. Wilder felt the air whirling behind him. He turned to see the triple tree's branches twisting like angry snakes. Wilder turned to run, but his legs were caught again in a nest of vines. They dug into his flesh, stung and burned him like fire ants. "Thistle, help me. Why are you just standing there?"

She stared past him, at the great knotted tree, at the swirling waters; then her eyes rested on him.

"You could say," she said, "in my way, I *am* helping you. This is one of the oldest, most sacred spots. Right now, you are in the intersection of the river and the tree. You are in the delta of civilizations, a place most dear to me, the place where I was born. Where I am seen."

Wilder flailed his arms in the water, legs rooted. "Listen, baby, I see you and you are so beautiful to me—I just need you to help me right now. See if you can help pull me up. I'm tangled in these weird vines. Some kind of bad storm is coming, and I think that old tree is about to fall down."

Wilder didn't like how she was looking. She was facing him, but her water-eddy eyes seemed to peer through him, focusing on something else. Wilder felt more wind at his back. The air filled with the rustling of leaves and needles, the sound of a hundred cicadas, a humming buzzing sound that rattled his ears, jarred his teeth.

Thistle closed her eyes and nodded her head. She opened them, a peaceful smile on her face as she crouched before him. "I like to believe in balance, in the natural order of things. I take from life, and I like to think that I'm giving life as well." She reached above him. Wilder gripped her arm.

"Thistle, please," he hissed. He leaned forward and stroked her cheek, his muddy fingers caressing her hair. "I don't know what's happening, but I need you—"

"You don't see me," she said. "Even now. You never did." Thistle jerked out of his grip. A clump of black hair fell away in Wilder's hand. He stared, his breath shallow.

"Thistle, what's wrong?" he whispered. He held the hair for a moment, then let it drop into the water. It floated like a feather. "Are you sick? Why didn't you tell me? Is that why you wanted me to meet your mother? How long have you known?"

His mind was racing, panic spreading. If she had cancer, he thought he could deal. *Maybe.* He wanted to hold her, but he couldn't get out of the water. He was pulling with all his strength, and the vines that held him barely budged. *Why did he have to find out like this?*

"You're going to have to try, baby, to pull me, or go for help. I can't stay out here, not like this."

Thistle's eyes were on the hair that still floated on the skin of water. Her hands flew to her scalp.

"Damn," she said. She held her hands up. Her nails were gone. She slipped her silver rings off and tossed them into the water next to Wilder. They sank with tiny little bubbles. The nail on her index finger dangled by a thread of cuticle. No blood, just dry, flaking skin. The air hummed again, a whispering sound like many rushing waters. "I know, Mama," she whispered. "I know."

"Thistle, stop it." Sickness and anger rose to his throat. "Your nails are falling off. You're falling apart, and you're talking crazy!" He swallowed, covered his mouth with a muddy fist, lowered his voice. "What kind of cancer do you have?" She frowned at him, stared. Wilder shook his head, tried to make sense of Thistle's decay. *How could she hurt like that and not bleed?* "You wouldn't accept chemo, no matter what the doctors said, so that means you've been trying to fight it naturally this whole time?" He closed his eyes. "That's why you've been eating all that weird shit?" *But her hair, her hair fell out in his hand.* He shook his head, confused. "Baby, I'm so sorry. Why didn't you tell me?"

Wilder jerked and strained in the mud, trying to walk. He clawed at the sediment and silt, his legs struggling underwater. For a moment he felt the vines loosen from his knees then creep up his legs again, holding him still. The vines pricked and stung him more, held him tighter. Everywhere they touched him, his skin felt itchy and scaly, as if sunburned. His legs began to feel heavy, leaden. He tried to reach for Thistle, but her eyes looked different. They caught the silver light, giving her face an eerie amber glow. Her skin was ashen, her cheeks hollow.

Thistle stared in the space above his head, as if she hadn't heard anything he'd said. Wilder looked up to see one of the knotted tree's long thick branches hovering above him. He froze. Thistle picked seven bell-like yellow blossoms from the limb and held them in her open palms. An invitation.

Wilder shook his head no, but Thistle kissed him, her mouth filled with tiny razor-like teeth. He tried to pull back, but he felt sleepy. Her tongue was sweet, like honey and mead, and she held him as she always did and whispered to him, the songs that only she could sing, with words that only she remembered the meaning to. His eyes grew bleary, and he heard more than he ever had—the croak of the plump, brown toad beneath an unfurled leaf, the jewel beetle scuttling across algae-covered bark, and the wind in the leaves, the many hundred leaves rustling above his head and a chorus of crickets.

Thistle smelled of maple syrup and buttermilk, of wet grass and rain-soaked walking sticks, of a wet stone covered by moss and babbling brook. Her eyes were too round, too full of silver and purple-golden light. Her skin was riven by deep whorls and lines, as if it had been carved with a knife.

When Thistle fed him the seven bells, Wilder's mouth was still full with the taste of sweet nectar, but then the blossoms stung the inside of his jaw, and the tip of his tongue went numb. He stared at her, struggled to keep his thoughts clear, to make his lips and teeth form words. Only shallow gasps escaped, a jaw harp deflated, out of tune. Recognition clouded his eyes. Wilder's heart was brittle, ready to break.

As the poison flowed through him, he felt the hum of a strange touch; fallen roots blossomed in electric earth. He was being lifted, carried backward through the waters.

"Don't struggle," Thistle called to him. "Mama just wants to meet you."

As the vines covered him, the limbs pulling him closer to the great tree's bosom, Wilder felt pieces of himself, like pieces of dusk, fall apart and be gathered in the bark and dirt. Thistle was naked. Now he could see her—a body no longer woman but willowy tree. Her bright round forehead shone in the moonlight. Her skin was tattooed with the whorls and swirling textures found on old-growth trees. Snails and mussels clung to her legs. Flowering vines and green moss wrapped around her thighs. Wilder thought he saw blue mountains, perhaps galaxies flowing in her ancient hair that now fell away in clumps like riverweed and algae at her feet. If he could move he would have reached for her. He would have tasted her with his fingertips and tongue, but she was out of reach. He wanted to cringe, to creep away. He wanted to lean into his lover's palms. He couldn't do either, so Wilder no longer tried to move.

His eyes asked the question his lips could not.

"People are the cancer," she said as she flicked an emerald beetle from her shoulder and followed him into the muddy pit. "Not all of them, of course, but enough of the wrong ones to wreck the balance. The movement needs people with heart," she said. "Spirits committed to systemic solutions, long-game change," she said. "But that's not you, is it, Wilder? At least not yet."

Wilder felt his breath grow short. Where each began, a tickling fire flowed through his blood. Seven thousand songs surged from stones as Thistle walked over to him. In the ghostly light she still looked almost human, beautiful. Wilder's ears hummed. Alarm, desire, and fear echoed in his temples, a competing heartbeat.

She embraced him, smelled like the strange, yellow blossoms.

Thistle caressed his throat with a sandpaper tongue; the skin peeled off in gentle flakes like wet dark bark. "I told you Mama would love, love you…" Her voice was airy, a solemn fractal, whispery as the wind. Wilder craned his neck to reach for her. The fragrant pheromones released from the tree dulled his pain, mixed it with his hunger. Even in the face of his dwindling energy, the memory of life fading fast, desire welled inside him; however, Thistle had completely transformed. She was no longer recognizable, and he was no longer sure how he could love her, but he did.

He remained still as a rock in a river of sound as Thistle and her Mama pulled apart the disparate shreds of who he used to be. In their presence, his thoughts felt noisy, cluttered. He tried to clear his throat to speak, but he could not feel it or his mouth. A gurgle and a rush of air escaped the hole where his throat and esophagus used to be. If he were a pipe, she could have played him. Wilder the bone harp, the baddest instrument in the world.

Thistle gently ran her fingers across his chest, then ripped his tank off. His eyes widened. "Don't worry,

Wilder," she said, her lips and sawteeth stained blood red, his back sinking into the smooth base of the knotted tree. Mama licked him, and he sensed another part of himself slide away. A spine of bones exposed to the night's air, he thought he could hear pieces of the old flesh drop into the waters, remnants of his former selves sink into the muck, but he was no longer certain if he still had ears.

"The Tupelo, Black Gum tree has a strong heartwood," Thistle said. "It's one of the oldest native trees here, like the oaks, and the poplars, but, of course, not as old as Mama. And you've probably guessed, Mama is not from around here. She came with the river. But Wilder, you'll have plenty of time to contemplate the true meaning of change. Mama will keep you company. She'll sing you the old songs and tell you her stories. She'll keep you safe with the others until—"

Brambles curved around his chin. Thorns pierced his flesh while he tasted her final honeysuckled kiss. His thoughts disappeared in the rising mist. Wilder's mind rang with a new truth. He would die here. Perhaps he would be reborn. To spring from the earth, a fresh green shoot, dark roots twisting deep beneath the river's belly. A sapling tree, straining for the scent of rain, reaching for change. Wilder felt as if he had traveled through a dream, as if he woke beneath a river and there was no way back through the forest except to become clear water, a spring to fill and heal himself. His eyes wide awake, his body unable to move, his fear vanished into the dark center of things. As Wilder watched over Thistle's shoulder, her tiny teeth sinking into his cheek, he saw where she had dropped the first gift he had made for her, into the bubbling earth. Muddy watery fingers reached in languid waves to snatch the jacket up. The world afar,

the last spike floated
in dark womb-water, shimmered
a sinking star.

Author Biography

Sheree Renée Thomas is the author of *Shotgun Lullabies: Stories & Poems* and the editor of two World Fantasy Award-winning anthologies, *Dark Matter: A Century of Speculative Fiction from the African Diaspora* and *Dark Matter: Reading the Bones*, featuring the works of beloved pioneers, celebrated, and new, emerging writers who continue to make valuable contributions to the field. Her work has been anthologized in *Stories for Chip: Tribute to Samuel* R. *Delany, Memphis Noir, A Moment of Change: Feminist Speculative Poetry, The Ringing Ear: Black Poets Lean South, So Long Been Dreaming: Postcolonial Science Fiction & Fantasy, Mojo: Conjure Stores, 80! Memories & Reflections on Ursula K. Le Guin, Bum Rush the Page: A Def Poetry Jam,* and other books. In 2015 she served as the Lucille Geier Lakes Writer-in-Residence at Smith College, and received the Wallace Foundation Fellowship at the Millay Colony of the Arts, as well as fellowships at the Blue Mountain Center and VCCA. In 2016 she was named a Tennessee Arts Fellow in Creative Writing by the Tennessee Arts Commission. She has also received fellowships from Cave Canem, Writers Omi/Ledig House, and the New York Foundation for the Arts. A native of Memphis, Thomas writes between a river and a pyramid.